ON THE ROADS OF WAR

ON THE ROADS OF WAR

A Soviet Cavalryman on the Eastern Front

IVAN YAKUSHIN

Translated and edited by: Bair Irincheev
English text: Christopher Summerville

Pen & Sword
MILITARY

First published in Great Britain in 2005 by
Pen & Sword Military
An imprint of Pen & Sword Books Ltd
47 Church Street
Barnsley
South Yorkshire
S70 2AS

ISBN 1 84415 144 1

Typeset in Sabon by Phoenix Typesetting,
Auldgirth, Dumfriesshire
Printed and bound in England by
CPI, UK

Pen & Sword Ltd incorporates the Imprints of Pen & Sword Aviation,
Pen & Sword Maritime, Pen & Sword Military, Wharncliffe Local
History, Pen & Sword Select, Pen & Sword Military Classics and
Leo Cooper.

For a complete list of Pen & Sword titles please contact
PEN & SWORD BOOKS LTD
47 Church Street, Barnsley, South Yorkshire, S70 2AS, England
E-mail: enquiries@pen-and-sword.co.uk
Website: www.pen-and-sword.co.uk

Contents

Author's Note

I am one of the last men from the 5th Guards Cavalry Division left alive. When I came to serve with the division in late 1943, I was one of the youngest officers in my regiment, and all those I knew and stayed in contact with after the war have passed away.

I arrived at the Front in May 1943, the turning year of the Great Patriotic War. I did not experience the bitterness and infamy of the defeats of 1941 and 1942. I was full of patriotism and eagerness to fight for my country. Thus, my view of the war is rather positive, due to my participation in the victorious offensive operations of the III Guards Cavalry Corps in Belorussia, Poland, and Germany. Despite receiving three wounds and shell-shock, I am a lucky man: I have survived and I am not a cripple.

Neither a journalist nor a writer, I should like to apologize for any shortcomings in style. I am a simple survivor of the Great Patriotic War. These are my memories.

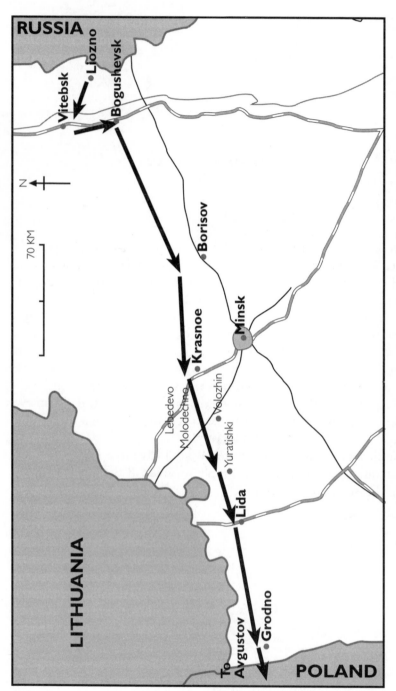

The Route of the 5th Guards Cavalry Division across Belorussia

RUSSIA

Liozno

Vitebsk

Bogushevsk

N

70 KM

Borisov

Minsk

Krasnoe

Lebedevo

Molodechno

Volozhin

Yuratishki

Lida

LITHUANIA

Grodno

To Avgustov

POLAND

A Lull in the Air

The forest was dark. The firefight did not abate. The sound of shooting came closer and closer. All of a sudden, a Soviet soldier ran into the clearing in front of me. He lifted his sub-machine gun and fired a long burst into the air. I shouted: 'Stop! Where are the Germans?' The soldier was dumbfounded. Only when he saw me, there in bushes, did he shout back with joy and jubilation: 'What Germans? Victory! Victory!' He fired several more bursts into the air before running off to tell his comrades the great news. We were all waiting for victory, but we did not expect it would come so quickly and so unexpectedly. I crawled back into the building, back into the room. It was empty but for the second badly wounded man who could not walk, and who was hiding under his bed. I returned my pistol to its lair in the map case. Then I began to shout: 'Hurrah! Hurrah! Victory! Victory . . .'

*   *   *

My studies were over. After completing school exams in spring 1941, I was on summer holiday. I had one more year left in school. After a brief discussion, our family decided to spend the summer in our Fatherland, in the Tula region, on the shores of our beloved River Oka. After shopping for gifts for our relatives there, we – my mother, my younger brother Nikolai, and I – were on the train. After changing trains twice, once at Vitebsk and again at Smolensk, we arrived in Belev, an ancient Russian town. Belev is older than Moscow and there are still some remains of mediaeval fortifications left in town. The buildings are mostly one- and two-storey structures, painted white, fitting the name of the town well: Belev is a derivative from the Russian adjective *bely*, meaning 'white'.

Aunt Ustinya, my mother's sister, met us at the station (we had sent her a telegram from Leningrad, warning of our arrival). Aunt Ustinya lived and worked in Belev, not far from the station. We stayed overnight at her place and were later picked up by Uncle Alex. He took us to his village, Zubkovo, some 30 kilometres from Belev, on the border of the Orel region. The village was located next to a postal railway station named Doltsy. This was the place where we were planning to spend our summer holiday, visiting other relatives in the nearby villages of Nikolaevka and Bedrintsy. We had to visit all our relatives and stay at least a little while with each of them – otherwise they would have been offended. The brick house where I was born was still standing in Bedrintsy (our father took my mother and me to Leningrad when I was eighteen months old), occupied by my father's brother, Uncle Peter, and his family.

The summer of 1941 was warm, sunny and generous for fruits. Fresh air, fresh milk, fragrance of herbs, forests, orchards, and meetings with relatives . . . all these things made our holiday excellent. Our life in the big city was left behind and our world shrank to a summer rest in my native countryside. We fished, played with cousins of our age, swam in crystal waters, and sunbathed on golden sandy beaches. This is how we were spending our early summer in 1941. An unstable world situation and war on the Western Front did not bother us much. The complicated political games and the non-aggression pact with Germany calmed simple people and created an illusion of stability and safety. There was a lull in the air, as before a storm.

The first two weeks of June quickly passed by. Then worrying rumours began circulating from village to village. One woman said there was a troll living under her stove, and this troll told her that great grief and misery was about to strike the whole population. The womenfolk nodded and sighed, but the peasant men just laughed at yet another stupid rumour: yet they, too, felt uneasy . . .

The war started on 22 June 1941. It arrived suddenly, like a storm in a clear blue sky. A hasty mobilization started. First Communists, then simple peasants, began lining up in front of drafting stations. My Uncle Alex (Alexei Titovich Pankin) was also drafted into the Army. He had just returned from the Winter War against Finland

[November 1939 to March 1940 – editor's note]. He had been a member of the Communist Party since 1918, but the only privilege the Communists had at the Front was receiving the first bullets from the enemy: for they were honoured with leading our assaults. I remember I took the news of the war quite calmly, just like most young people of those days. We were so assured of the invincibility of our Red Army that we thought the Germans would be thrown out of the country in a matter of weeks. But as I followed the news reports, telling of the advance of German armies into Russia, my opinion changed.

Women started weeping and crying. Replacement companies marched through Doltsy train station. The soldiers – exhausted and covered with dust – stayed in the shadow of the tall trees near the post office. They were re-rolling their foot rags and leg wrappings, and drinking cold water from wells. Some stout older women, and we teenagers, brought buckets full of water to the soldiers, and many peasant girls gave them eggs, milk, bread, tobacco – wiping away tears.

The news from the Front was worrying. The official reports of the *Sovinformbureau* were just as depressing. Despite putting up stubborn resistance, the Red Army was surrendering one town after another to the Germans. The front line was quickly approaching Leningrad, drawing nearer and nearer to our village. I tried to convince my mother we had to leave, otherwise we would fall under German occupation. In my opinion, we had to make it to our father, to Leningrad, by all possible means. Belev and the surrounding villages could be surrendered to the Germans but not Leningrad! I was firm about this. Eventually my mother agreed and we started packing for our journey. We had to say goodbye to our relatives in all four villages. I volunteered for this mission and travelled to all by bicycle. I arrived back home after midnight completely exhausted. My mother and younger brother had not been wasting time: I found them hastily packing. Our relatives killed and fried chicken for us, baked some pies, boiled eggs, packed lard and bread for us. They knew our trip would be long and hard. They were seeing us off with tears in their eyes. Would we ever see them again?

The front line was approaching central Russia and no one was sure if it would not reach Moscow by winter. The Germans did not spare civilians in the occupied territories. My cousins, Ivan and Alex

Pankin, were preparing to join a local partisan unit (and this they did, fighting bravely and falling like heroes, in battle, in 1942).

Early in the morning we gathered all our belongings and left the village. Our aunts and cousins saw us off all the way to the main road. They were weeping and crying, hugging my mother, sobbing for their men, who had already left for the Front. They were mourning them as if they were already dead. It took some effort to finally pull ourselves away. We then hitched a ride to Belev in a horse-drawn carriage, covering the first 30 kilometres of our journey.

In Belev we again stayed with Aunt Ustinya. She worked at the railway station and we hoped to buy tickets to Leningrad through her. Despite all her efforts, however, no tickets could be got for Leningrad – not even for Moscow. It was impossible to buy them, as they were simply not sold. Eventually, and with great difficulty, we managed to buy tickets for Tula. After a brief farewell to Aunt Ustinya, we started our journey to Tula in an overcrowded train.

There were crowds of people at the station in Tula, trying to travel in different directions. Civilian passengers queued at ticket offices for hours, even days. The road to Moscow was closed. Only military personnel could get tickets to Moscow with the written permission of the station chief. I tried to find companions travelling to Leningrad in this swarm of people. And indeed, I found a young man of my age, Boris, a student of the 7th Special Artillery School in Leningrad. With his school ID in hand, dressed in his cadet uniform, he was trying to buy tickets to Moscow, but in vain. He could buy a ticket for himself, but he was not alone – there were his mother, aunt, and ten-year-old cousin travelling with him. They were on their way from Kiev and had got stuck in Tula. We made a deal and decided to go to Leningrad together. We quickly introduced all our relatives to each other, gathered them all on one spot, and took command of our group. We had to find a way out of the situation. Our relatives gave us some money and we bought some more food for the journey. As the route through Moscow was closed, we decided to travel around it, bypassing it from the east via Ryazhsk, Ryazan, Yaroslavl, Vologda, Cherepovets, Tikhvin and Volkhov.

We journeyed on both passenger and freight trains. On the latter, we travelled in the open air, sitting on the cargo platforms (in spite of a strict ban, punishable by execution). During our journey, we came under attack from German dive bombers, but we stubbornly continued towards our goal. On both sides of the track we could see broken up, burnt out steam engines and wagons. Sometimes, during the attacks of these German hawks, our train would stop and we would jump out head first, taking only money and IDs with us. After the Germans had had their share of 'fun', strafing and bombing the train, we would return to our places and continue the journey. If the dive bombers and fighters only strafed us, firing their machine-guns, the train would not stop, and we, like soldiers at the Front, would have to experience the pleasure of listening to bullets whizzing, whining, and ricocheting. The closer we got to Leningrad, the more we were attacked by the German Air Force.

After several more days we were in Tikhvin, and in several hours, Volkhov. But that was it. There were no more trains going to Leningrad, as the Germans had cut the rail link. The German Air Force raided the railway station often, and we would all hide in foxholes, dug right in the centre of the square in front of the station building. The station chief told us that two armoured trains were departing for Leningrad. If these armoured trains managed to break through, ordinary trains would start running again. Next day, one of the two armoured trains came back. The link was not re-established. Our women lost heart. Boris's mother proposed we should stay in some village for the time being. She could work as a school teacher, while everyone else found jobs on a *kolkhoz* [a collective farm – editor's note]. We would stay there until the Germans were repelled and the road to Leningrad was reopened.

Such were the conversations we were having, when news came of a column of military trucks, due to arrive from Leningrad. Boris and I immediately found this column. After a conversation with a captain – the commander of the column – it turned out the trucks brought bread from Leningrad and were supposed to return to the city in one day. We asked him to take us with him. He agreed at first, but when he heard there were women and children with us, he bluntly refused. We offered him a lot of money and all sorts of assistance, but he would not give in. He refused to take any money from us. It was only after we had really worn him down, working on his nerves, that he finally agreed to take us all, on the condition we would constantly scan the skies, and warn the drivers of any approaching enemy aircraft. We gladly agreed.

We departed from Volkhov before dawn. Boris and his relatives were in the trunk of the first truck, while my mother, younger brother, and I, were in the last truck. The column was driving on some small forest roads. When we approached a clearing, we would start searching the sky. We were lucky. It was cloudy and there were no German planes in sight. Late in the evening, we arrived in Leningrad and drove to Moscow Station. It was already curfew and we could not walk in the city without a pass. Boris's mother proposed we stayed overnight at their place, as they lived close by. Their flat was empty. There was a letter from Boris's father, saying that he had been drafted into the Red Army and had gone to the Front. We slept on the floor without taking off our clothes, as we had not washed ourselves for many days. Still, it felt great, as we were home, in Leningrad.

Black Soil Sweetened by Sugar

Our father did not expect to see us, as Leningrad was almost completely surrounded and cut off from the rest of the country. Father was about to go to work when we all entered the flat with our luggage. Unluckily, our arrival coincided with the introduction of rationing, and a shortage of food could already be sensed in the city. One could still buy some soup or porridge without rationing cards in a small canteen on the corner of Ogorodnikova and Lermontovski Prospekts, but all other canteens required rationing cards. After some trouble, we also managed to get rationing cards.

Schools did not work. Most of my friends were working as assistants at various factories. I was sixteen years old. Those who were seventeen managed to volunteer for *opolchenie* [Home Guard – editor's note] divisions. My friend Sergei Yegorov was strutting around in the fancy uniform of the 9th Special Artillery School, which was preparing cadets for studies in military academies. His uniform was beautiful: a tunic with two crossed cannon barrels on the collar tabs, dark blue trousers with red piping, boots, tailored greatcoat, visor cap, and a belt with a bronze buckle adorned with a star. This uniform was an object of jealousy for all the teenage boys in the building. Sergei and another *'Spets'* (the nickname given to students of special artillery schools) convinced me to apply to their 9th Special Artillery School.

The end of the war was far away, and we all realized we would have to fight: better, then, to fight after a military education; to fight as an officer rather than an enlisted man. I tried to convince my friends, Pavel Petrov, Boris Karamazin, and Sergei Zorin, to apply for the same artillery school. Only Sergei Zorin agreed, and applied to the 9th Special Artillery School together with me. We had to attend a medical inspection. I was afraid they would not accept me because of my weak eyes, so I asked Sergei Zorin to go through the eye inspection twice, the second time with my papers. The eye doctor was either tired or absent-minded, and did not notice our cheating. So we were accepted into the 1st Platoon, 1st Battery, of the 9th Special Artillery School, which was equivalent to the 10th year of regular secondary school. We were issued military uniforms and observed military formalities, such as saluting officers we met in the street.

On 8 September 1941, German troops completely surrounded Leningrad and the siege began. Nevertheless, our classes continued. Along with general educational courses, we studied field manuals, the basics of artillery science, and did a lot of drill. Our school commander was an Armenian, Captain Khachaturyan. He had a problem with Russian language and pronounced some words in a very funny way, but he was a really good commander and was respected by both students and teachers in the school. I heard that in 1942 he left the school, went to the Front, and served as a commander of an artillery regiment.

Before the cold weather set in we marched a lot, goose-stepping on Moskvina Prospekt to Izmailovski Prospekt and back. Sometimes we would march around Trinity Cathedral. When winter came, marching in the streets stopped. Heating in the school building no longer worked, so we sat in our classes wrapped up in greatcoats. But despite cold and hunger, we continued to study the basics of military science. Of all foreign languages we studied only German. When a teacher entered a classroom, the student on duty would report to him in German.

One day in September, I received an official letter from a local *Komsomol* (Lenin's Youth Organization) section, inviting me to come to their office. I reported to them and waited for further orders. But there were no orders! The *Komsomol* secretary looked at my military uniform, took the official letter, apologized, and said there must have been a mistake and I was free to go. Apparently, they did not know I had entered the Special Artillery School and thought I was sitting at home, doing nothing.

School was important, but equally important was getting more food for my family, especially for my mother and younger brother Nikolai. They did not work and they both received a minimal amount of bread. We realized too late that we had to get extra food for winter. We felt the approach of hunger. One day, however, before Strelna was captured by the Germans, Sergei Yegorov and I managed to make a trip there and bring back a bag of potatoes each. It happened in the following way . . .

On 5 September 1941, we took two empty bags and went to Strelna by tram (my cousin Marusya lived there with her family and before the war I would sometimes stay at her place during the summer). From the window of the tram we did not see any fortifications or defence works, and the vehicle was full of civilians who were all calm. We got off the tram at the last stop and walked westwards, down Old Peterhof Road. We did not get to see Marusya. Instead, we turned into a potato field and ran into an artillery battery in firing positions. A senior lieutenant – apparently the commanding officer of the battery – was running back and forth giving orders. When he saw us, he started shouting, telling us to get out: 'Go away! go away!' We were dressed in the uniform of the Special Artillery School, with artillery emblems on our collar tabs. Owing to this, we managed to negotiate a deal with the commander, and he permitted us to dig some potatoes next to his battery: 'Dig the potatoes, but in fifteen minutes you must get out from here!' The potatoes were excellent and we filled our bags to the brim. After that we slowly walked to the tram stop. There were a lot of people there but the tram did not show up. We waited for about half an hour, and then decided to hitch-hike. A military truck we stopped took us to the Obvodny Channel, and from there it was only three tram stops to my home. Everyone at home was excited and happy when they saw the bag of potatoes. The next day Strelna was captured by German troops. But the potatoes helped us to last through the winter.

In November 1941 we also went to the cabbage fields in Ozerki to find frozen cabbage leaves and roots: but they were of little nutritional value. We also arrived too late at the ruins of the Badayevski food warehouse, which burnt down during the first massive German air raid on 8 September 1941. All we found there was black soil sweetened by sugar, which had melted during the fire. We owned a cat – which was fat before the war – but of course it went missing in November: someone ate it.

Hunger took a tight grip of our family. I was better off, as I received rations in the canteen at the artillery school, and I had an Army ration card. But my mother and brother had civilian ration cards, which gave only 125 grams of bread per day. My father had a worker's ration card.

We had to find a way to survive. One night my father had a brilliant idea. He used to work as a supply manager for a bone powder plant, and he knew the location of all the rubbish pits where restaurants and canteens dumped bones. He decided to check those places and look for some bones. To our joy, he found some bones in frozen soil. My mother boiled the bones in a large pot, and collected the fat that melted from them into small jars. There was even a little meat left on the bones. Our whole family gnawed the bones for dinner. It was a real feast! The bone fat my mother collected helped them to survive through the most awful days of the siege.

During the winter of 1941–1942 death was wiping out the citizens of Leningrad with lightning speed. I remember how one day I helped a completely exhausted gentleman to get over a lump of snow in the street. I did not see his face, as it was covered with a scarf: but I saw him on the way back from my school – he was lying dead in the street on the corner of Maklin and Sadovaya Streets, outside a pharmacy. The scarf had fallen from his face, revealing an unshaved, worn out countenance. I walked past his corpse every day. No one had energy to remove corpses from the streets. Just like that, the citizens of Leningrad were quietly dying of hunger, one by one, giving their lives for their city. Snow soon covered the old man's body, transforming it into a small, silver-white hillock.

My father had a light carriage with large wheels from pre-war times. It was standing chained in the courtyard. After my evacuation father summoned his remaining strength and made a living by transporting goods and firewood to the shops, receiving bread or other food as payment. My mother found work in the summer of 1942, after my younger brother was evacuated from Leningrad and their life became a little better. They also received a small plot of land next to the Kirovski Plant and one potato to start with. They grew a whole potato field from this one potato. In 1946, when I came back from the Army, we dug up thirty big bags of potatoes and some other vegetables from that field. But that was in 1946, while in the winter of 1941–1942 people were dropping like flies from hunger.

My classes in the Special Artillery School continued, but extreme cold, hunger, air raids, and artillery bombardments often frustrated my attempts to study. In late January 1942 we students disassembled wooden houses for firewood, but as we grew weaker with every day, dystrophy [a deficiency in the nourishment of a part of the body – editor's note] finally got us: our bodies swelled from drinking too much water.

The following relatives of mine died of hunger in Leningrad during the winter 1941–1942:

> My uncle Ivan Ivanovich Yakushin, born in 1873
> His wife, Anastasia Yakushina, born in 1880
> Their daughter, Maria Yakushina, born in 1924
> Their daughter, Evdokiya Yakushina, born in 1920 (her body was never found)
> My second uncle Timofey Yakushin, born in 1878

So the entire family of my uncle Ivan Yakushin died of hunger during the first and the most horrible winter of the siege. Ivan Yakushin was the older brother of my father, so my father had to take care of his funeral. There was a small marketplace next to Trinity Church, where we used to march with our Special Artillery School. During the winter of 1941–1942 the marketplace was converted into a morgue. Dead bodies were lying there in stacks. My father made some sort of a coffin, a mere wooden box, for his older brother and brought the body there on a small sledge. Several morgue workers were warming themselves at the fire. When my father brought the body of his brother in the coffin, the morgue workers pulled the body of Ivan Yakushin out of the box and put it into the common stack of bodies, and threw the improvised coffin into the fire, thanking my father for bringing them firewood. I do not know how my father took care of the other dead relatives. According to my wife, who survived the siege as a teenager, there were trucks driving around the city picking up dead bodies, but I never saw such trucks.

There were rumours circulating in the city about cannibalism, but I personally saw nothing connected with it. When we had political classes in our Special Artillery School, the *politruk* (political officer) told us that cannibals were executed regardless of their hunger or position in society. I do not know if this was true or not. My wife later told me she saw bodies of children in the streets that were missing legs or arms, but I personally did not see such things.

My father was a simple worker, who had taken part in the First World War and was taken prisoner by the Germans. He was not a member of the Communist party: he was just an ordinary Russian person. However, even from him, I never heard any comments about surrendering the city to the Germans. All he said to us was that we had to hold on and survive the siege and the war.

Our house at 160 Griboyedova Channel had belonged to the Pokrovskaya Church before the revolution. We had different people living in the building, both respectable persons from the pre-revolution upper classes who lived in separate flats, and simple working people who shared communal flats with each other. We lived peacefully and in good relations with all neighbours; we knew everyone and tried to help everyone, if it was necessary. In our whole large apartment block there was only one alcoholic, a painter named Belkin, but he was quiet. When he was sober, he worked very quickly, so we all tried to invite him for painting jobs in our flats.

Before the war there was a very good bomb and gas shelter built in the basement of our building. It was completely insulated, and had a ventilation system, chemical filters, and very strong steel doors. When the war broke out, all those who had not left for the Front, received gas masks and were told to cover their windows with blankets and put paper strips on them as well. We took turns on duty during air raids, standing at the entrance of the shelter and on the roof. Germans dropped a lot of termite incendiary bombs on the city. The men of the local civil defence units (MPVO), many of them still children and teenagers, had to take the termite bombs with special pincers and throw them into a box filled with sand, or just throw them into the street from the roof.

But human beings get used to everything – even to daily air raids and shelling. The occupants of the building eventually became quite lazy about going down to the shelter every time a siren sounded. The MPVO units dragged anyone they could find in the street into a shelter during an air raid, but they could not control people who just stayed in their flats. Despite the dangerous proximity of the Marti Plant, which was always targeted by German bombers, on that cursed day, 30 October 1941, my mother and my brother Nikolai decided to chance their luck, and did not leave the flat when the siren sounded. They were hoping our building would not get hit. Every day when I returned from school after yet another air raid, I was nervous: 'What if our house got hit? It is so close to the Marti Plant! What would happen to my family then?' On that day I was especially restless. On the way home, at Alarchin Bridge, I bumped into our neighbour, Elizabeth. Holding back tears, she told me our building had been hit by a bomb and my mother and brother had been taken to hospital. I ran to our building as fast as feet would carry me. The front wall, facing the channel, was intact: the heavy bomb had landed in the backyard. All the windows and doors were gone. There was a huge crater in the backyard, and walls were covered with deep cracks. Luckily, the staircases were undamaged, and I ran up to the first floor and into our flat. The flat was empty. Wind was blowing through it. Doors and windows were gone. All the furniture had been blown away and pressed into the main wall of the building by the blast of the explosion. 'How could my mother and Nikolai survive such an explosion? What happened to them? Where are they?'

In the backyard I found Aunt Nyusha, mother of my friend Sergei Yegorov. She was in charge of the bomb shelter and had sent all the wounded, including my mother and brother, to a hospital. She calmed me down, saying my mother and brother were lightly wounded; they would probably return from the hospital in a couple of weeks. When father came back from work he immediately went to the hospital, while I carried the surviving items to the bomb shelter. This was where we stayed for several days.

When my mother and brother came back from the hospital we already had a new flat on the same channel, in building number 156. My mother and brother had survived by a sheer miracle. When the bomb exploded my mother was on her knees, washing the floor near the window, protected by a thick brick wall. My brother was in the corridor, also protected by a wall. Mother was badly wounded in her back by glass splinters, flung into the room by the force of the blast. Her whole back was one big bloody mess, and the surgeons had a hard time removing the tiny splinters. My brother received a slight splinter wound in his head.

Many buildings were damaged and destroyed in our district. The next building on Griboyedova Channel, No. 154, was hit twice. While standing on duty during the air raid, I saw the first bomb hit that building. Meanwhile, a heavy shell hit Alarchin Bridge and went through it. During the same artillery barrage our neighbour and relative of my future wife, military engineer Nikolai Fedorov, was mortally wounded by a splinter and died in the street, in my mother's arms. His wife, Lubov Fedorova, died of hunger during the winter that followed.

On New Year's Eve 1942, all the students of the 9th Special Artillery School were invited to the Gorky Theatre for a performance. Despite the most awful frosts, we maintained strict military discipline and wore the same uniform as usual: greatcoat, tunic, dark blue trousers with red piping and boots. The frozen hall of the theatre was as cold as the streets outside. We sat in the hall in our greatcoats, shivering with cold. Our feet were especially frozen, but we tried not to stamp our boots and follow the performance on stage. It was Chekhov's *Cherry Orchard*. Actors, wrapped in fur coats, played their roles with great heroism and inspiration – the actors themselves were pale and thin from hunger and cold. May Anton Chekhov and the actors forgive us, but our minds were far away from the anxieties of Ranevskaya, the passing of her small world, and the death of old Firs. How could this tragedy be compared with our tragedy? Firs, the main character of the play, was dying old, while many of us were doomed to die young, if not in besieged Leningrad, then in battles at the Front. We saw people dying in the streets everyday, entire buildings falling into dust under German bombs and shells. But at the end of every act we clapped our hands and stamped our feet like crazy: it was an opportunity to warm our frozen feet and hands a little bit. I think everyone – both the spectators and the actors – were looking forward to the end of the performance, as we had all been invited for a *hot dinner*. Nothing could compare to a hot dinner for the hungry, cold, dystrophic inhabitants of Leningrad. It was the ultimate bliss. We did not think about anything else. It was just us and the food. Everything else was unimportant.

So, finally, the performance was over. Applause! Platoon by platoon, we march into the lobby of the theatre, where tables were ready for us. The dinner consisted of three courses: hot soup, a cutlet with pasta, and a fruit jelly for dessert. We were all issued a small chocolate bar – 'Golden Anchor' – to take home with us. No one expected such a feast. It was a luxurious treat and we were warmed both in our bodies and souls.

After the dinner we all walked home, hiding our precious chocolate bars in our breast pockets. We walked one by one on a narrow path, in deep snow, on the right shore of the River Fontanka. We could hear artillery fire in the distance, but here, in the city, it was completely quiet. There were no lights, no pedestrians. The city looked dead. The full moon in the sky was the only source of illumination during that night. All of us students, who survived the war and the siege, remembered this New Year's Eve of 1942 for the rest of our lives.

Promised Land

They started to speak about evacuating us as early as January 1942. The weakest among us, students, started to die from dystrophy. Most of us were swollen from swallowing water instead of food, in order to fill up our stomachs. This disease could easily be detected from the small depressions that remained in one's skin if one pressed on a swollen hand. These depressions would only disappear gradually.

The country needed to evacuate the *Spets* from artillery schools in order to train them and replace the losses of officers in the Army. Evacuation from Leningrad also gave us a chance to survive. The day of evacuation finally came. We were allowed to take warm clothes and *valenki* [felt boots – editor's note] with us. Only our mothers came to see us off, our fathers were all working in the factories or fighting at the Front. We were issued 700 grams of bread for the journey. While waiting for the transport to arrive, I began biting small pieces, until the bread was all gone. I was still hungry, and began to worry about what I would eat during the journey, which could last a long time. The very next morning I was sorry I had not given this bread to my mother, as we all had food and bread enough after crossing to the other shore of Lake Ladoga, while our relatives, who remained inside the ring of the siege, had very few chances of survival.

Our mothers were both happy and sad for us. They were happy because they knew we would not die from hunger, but sad because we were parting from them. Would we ever see each other again? They had to survive the siege; we had to survive the Front. It was war! And there was no end in sight. Germans were still standing at the gates of Moscow.

We were taken to Finland Station and loaded on a local train. They put so many students into the carriages that in several minutes there was no air left to breathe. In order to get some fresh air we shot at the windows from our small-calibre rifles. However, this did not help much until the train started moving.

There were trucks waiting for us on the shore of Lake Ladoga. We were sat on benches in the open backs of the trucks, saving every single place. It was dark. A blizzard was raging. We pressed our bodies against each other, trying to preserve at least a little bit of the warmth we had left from the train journey. I was sitting on the bench closest to the edge of the truck, next to the driver's cabin. We were sitting with our backs forward. A strong wind was blowing through my greatcoat and seemed to penetrate my body to the bones. I clenched my teeth so they would not chatter, and tried to recall the words of my mother: 'in Siberia they will feed you with white wheat bread and as much sweet pastry as you could wish.'

We were driving without any stops. Above us, was a dark sky with dry snowflakes falling from it; beneath was the white endless ice of the lake. After several kilometres the driver stepped on the brakes and made a sharp turn to the left from the road. Some truck in front of us was sinking through a hole in the ice. There were people crowding round it. The driver did not stop and came back to the main road. Everyone was silent.

A new life awaited us on the other side of Lake Ladoga. We drove up a small elevation, the truck stopped, and here we were on solid ground again. Nearby were some small wooden shacks that were not illuminated. We could detect the pleasant smell of a kitchen. 'Dismount!' The order came and we fell off the truck, numb to our bones from cold. We stretched our legs and cautiously walked to the gathering point. However, not all of us were destined to reach this Promised Land: one of the students, unable to stand the cold and hunger of the journey across the ice, died before reaching the shore. He opened a long list of *Spets* students who died during evacuation.

The dark buildings turned out to be a canteen and a waiting hall. It was warm inside. We could feel the hot food burning away the cold from our frozen bodies, giving energy to our muscles, and making us happier.

Our leaders received ration cards for the canteen, but many students tried to get an extra card by any means. This led them to death, for our main enemy at that moment was abundant fat food and overeating. Exhausted stomachs cannot digest such amounts of food: men started passing diarrhoea with blood, and this led to more deaths during our journey.

A freight train was waiting for us. We were to travel in cattle trucks with ramshackle bunk beds on both sides of the sliding doors. There was an iron stove in the middle of the wagon. We were the 1st Platoon of the 1st Battery, consisting of teenagers sixteen to seventeen years old. We were the oldest in the Special Artillery School and naturally we received less attention than the 2nd and the 3rd Batteries, who were even younger. 'Mount the train!' The order came and the wheels of the train began clattering on the rails.

The main shortcoming of a cattle truck is the absence of any sort of toilet. We were made particularly aware of this as our dystrophic stomachs were upset, and our train rarely stopped. At first, students simply suffered the pains in their stomachs, only emptying them during the brief stops, on the railway right next to our train. But the situation got much worse. Our train began stopping less and less frequently, and bloody diarrhoea took the lives of more and more *Spets* students. In the end, it was impossible to wait for stops, and students would open the sliding door and defecate while the train was moving at full speed.

Despite our situation, we did not lose our sense of humour. During one such defecating operation, *Spets* Petrov suddenly threw himself into the truck and shouted: 'Boys, I think I knocked down a telegraph pole with my arse!' When we looked out of the door, we saw a female railway worker with a small signal flag in her hand. She had slapped Petrov on his bare behind with the pole of this flag.

The weakest tried to stay next to the stove. But from this place they could only leave the truck dead or in a dying condition. I still remember the pose of those dying teenagers at the stove: arms outstretched and fingers spread wide, the better to grasp the heat. But one had to keep moving in order to survive: split firewood for the stove, walk around during stops, remove the dead from the train. And the main thing? Do not eat much!

During stops the station personnel always asked us: 'Are there any sick?' The answer was always positive. There were a lot of dead taken off the train, too. The station workers would take the dead and immobile students off the train. Most of these sick teenagers did not survive and their graves dotted the entire route of our journey.

Another victim of the stove was our platoon leader. This young lieutenant could not stand the test of the siege. He started speaking nonsense about how useful glass was for digestion, especially for dystrophic men. He told us we should eat anything made of glass! We turned him in to the station personnel at the next stop and he never came back to us.

When we reached the Urals, two mighty FD steam engines started pulling our train, which almost doubled our speed. There was a long stop in Novosibirsk. Sergei Zorin and I could not resist the temptation to go to the station canteen to eat some hot food. The canteen was cosy and the food was tasty, but our dystrophic stomachs could not take it. We both felt very sick after this, but we were saved by the fact the final destination of our journey was near.

We arrived in Mundy-Bash, a small town in the Altai Mountains. We were well received and accommodated in a warm light building, with all the conditions necessary for a fast recovery. Sergei and I spent about a week in a local hospital, then returned to the platoon. The food was excellent and we started to gain weight quickly in the clean mountain air. But although we gained fat quickly, the strength came back to our muscles quite slowly. Time was passing by and our classes started again.

Our classes were over in spring and we completed all the exams for the Maturity Certificate. Summer holiday started. Spring and summer are especially beautiful in the Altai Mountains, where nature is untouched. We could see Belukha, the highest mountain of Siberia, in the distance. There was a mine not far from us, and we could see trains full of ore going from there to the station. We did a lot of hiking in Taiga. During one of these hiking trips we found the hut of some Old Believers in a clearing. An old man who lived there greeted us, asking: 'Why are you youngsters wearing military uniforms?' He did not even know about the war. We were thirsty. He gave us water from his well, but as we were leaving, threw away the cup from which we had drunk. That was the tradition of the Old Believers, who did not use dishes 'desecrated' by another person. Our happy and carefree holiday quickly passed by.

Tomsk Artillery Academy

In August 1942 we, the 1st Battery, were sent to Tomsk, to the 1st Artillery Academy. On the way to Tomsk we stopped at Taiga railway station. We ate in a wooden canteen that looked more like a barrack. They served us mushrooms in large bowls, similar to those used in a steam bath. Despite the strangeness of the dishes in which the food was served, the mushrooms were delicious and we were happy and full for the rest of our journey.

We were accommodated outside the precincts of the 1st Artillery Academy in Tomsk. We were officially designated 'Candidate Cadets' and we spent about two weeks in this rank. Officers from different departments of the academy used our labour for all kinds of odd jobs, keeping us busy morning till night. We soon wearied of this, looking forward to the time when we could become real cadets and receive proper military uniforms.

I well remember one job we were given. One evening, we were detailed to unload logs from cargo ships on the River Tom'. The ship on which I worked was large and the logs were more than 1 metre in diameter. We were supposed to roll the logs to the sides of the ship and throw them into the water. It was quite dark: the searchlight barely illuminated our ship. I was expected to give my log a final push into water with a bar, but it was so thick I could not budge it. My friends were already rolling another log towards me so I had to hurry. Summoning all my strength, I kicked the log into the water, but was myself knocked off the ship by the next log. I plunged into the river from a height of 4 metres. During this descent I feared only one thing: that I would fall on a log and not into the water. But I was lucky and crashed into the river. I swam some 5 metres to the shore and walked back to the ship. I splashed into the captain's cabin, where our supervisor, a senior lieutenant, was making himself comfortable at a stove. He looked at me sternly, scolded me for carelessness at work, and ordered me to be back at work within fifteen minutes. I returned to my place on deck twenty minutes later in my wet uniform and continued rolling the logs. Happily, my uniform dried quickly: only my boots and socks remained soaking wet. Despite the cold ducking I did not catch 'flu.

Finally, the day of official enrollment came, and we were transferred to the barracks inside the Academy. We were issued new uniforms, *kirsa* boots, and greatcoats made of olive green English wool. These greatcoats were soft but too thin for Russian conditions (especially in Siberia). Finally, we were sworn in and issued with shoulder boards and belts (fastened by a brass buckle with a star on it).

Our course began with the main elements of garrison duty. We had to line up for morning and evening inspection many times, falling in at a moment's notice. They also checked our beds and uniforms – everything had to be in strict accordance with the manual. This was much harder than it sounds! After we were sworn in, classes started. They lasted eight hours a day. Four more hours were allotted for homework and preparation. We did our homework under the eye of a battalion officer, and we could not leave the place without his permission.

Our studies were combined with the regular duties of garrison service: guard duty, orderly duty, kitchen duty (the best thing about kitchen duty was peeling potatoes, as it was too hot near the huge pots where they cooked the food. It was also unpleasant to wash them, when one had to scramble inside, head over heels), and so on. All these duties were assigned according to a regular schedule. Those who broke the regulations were assigned extra duties out of turn. Sergeants were especially eager to assign extra duties to cadets. Barrack duty, for example, involved washing the huge floors in the barrack, guarding the properties in the barrack, and reporting on the location and tasks of a given battery or battalion.

It was better to be on guard duty, as the times for rest and sleep were strictly defined in the manual. The food was also better there. When we were on outdoor guard duty, in winter, we were issued with fur hats, felt boots, and sheepskin overcoats. We would stand with our collars turned up, warm and snug, even in temperatures of minus 50 degrees Celsius. But there was a danger of falling asleep. Court martial and duty at the Front in a penal battalion would be the best scenario for anyone who fell asleep on guard duty. So we walked back and forth to stay awake. Our battalion did not have any extraordinary situations, but the sister battalion had to court martial one cadet who fell asleep during guard duty.

We went to the steam bath at the edge of the city, mostly during time allocated for rest. On one occasion, we were preparing for sleep, having just returned from guard duty, when the order came: 'Reveille! Get up and march to the steam bath!' We were outraged, but fell in and marched. However, when the young senior lieutenant ordered, 'Sing!' we did not react. The lieutenant repeated the order five minutes later and again we were silent. Then the lieutenant ordered: 'Forward, run!' We ran. Then, 'Halt!' We halted. Then, 'Sing!' Nothing. Another run, another halt, another 'Sing!' order, but still we remained mute. A new order came: 'Down!' We dropped down in the dirt. 'Forward, crawl!' We crawled forward. There was a large pool of water on the road in front of us. We crawled into the muddy water and filth. 'Get up! Forward march!' All covered with muck, we marched into the steam bath. We deposited our clothes in a disinfection chamber and went to wash ourselves. We washed and changed our underwear, and then started to peel the dirt off our greatcoats and trousers. There was no 'Sing!' order on the way back. But when we approached the Academy, the senior lieutenant stopped the battery and gave an edifying speech, in which he said, among other things: 'What kind of sons of Leningrad are you? Have you not read, "How steel was hardened by Sholokhov?"' A roar of laughter from the cadets was the answer to his speech. That was the last time we saw this senior lieutenant: after this incident sergeant majors would take us to the steam bath.

The Siberian winter came with its famous frosts. The temperature was sometimes as low as minus 50 degrees Celsius. We were rolling 122 millimetre howitzers back and forth on the drill square in front of our barracks. It was difficult to assemble and disassemble the heavy guns in the cold: the heavy breech lock of a 152 millimetre howitzer could freeze onto the bare skin of one's hands. We also had a hard time during tactical training. We were freezing to our bones in the open Siberian fields in our thin English greatcoats. Only our legs stayed warm, in huge *valenki* felt boots. When frozen, these felt boots were so heavy one could easily kill a person with them. You could literally take them off and use them as a weapon in a hand-to-hand fight instead of a rifle.

Most of our training was concerned with artillery and military science: preparation of the fire mission data, calculation of co-ordinates for the fire mission, different types of artillery and small arms and their main battle characteristics, and so on. We also studied tactics and topography in depth, and a lot of attention was paid to drill. We studied both disciplinary and field manuals. And in addition to all this, we spent a lot of time doing tactical training in the field, during which we could see the cadets from the Belotserkovski Infantry Academy. Although we had it tough, they suffered even more. They had to sneak in deep snow, then storm dummy enemy positions with hand grenades and bayonets. In the hardest days of the Battle of Stalingrad, all these cadets from the Belotserkovski Infantry Academy were sent to the Front as an officer regiment. But we also had bayonet training: 'Short bayonet thrust – stab! Long bayonet thrust – stab!' We only had several hours of this training, however, while infantry cadets endured whole days and weeks of it.

Senior Sergeant Stulov was our deputy platoon leader. The degree of his inhumanity could only be compared with the degree of humanity and friendliness of our platoon leader, Lieutenant Serbin. Stulov was tall, wide-shouldered, and possessed extraordinary physical strength allied to an unusually bad personality. He could alone roll a 76 millimetre ZIS-3 cannon on the drill square. We did not know where this awful person came from. He had no friends. He maintained discipline in the platoon with brute force and a loud voice. He gave his commands in a mocking tone, like a torture-master, and if we failed to execute orders to his liking, he would make us repeat the task several times. He could find mistakes in anything: sewing on a button, covering a bed, polishing a belt buckle, cleaning boots. There was an endless list of things he could bitch about. But it was a great pleasure for him to make us repeat the same procedure over and over again.

We were ready to punish him with a 'dark beating' [an extreme form of protest and revenge in Russian military schools, in which a person is assaulted from behind, covered with a blanket that he might not see his attackers, and beaten up by the whole platoon or

company – editor's note] for all his tortures. But we thought better
of it, deciding instead to beat him up after graduating and becoming
officers. As Stulov was bad in all subjects but drill, there was no
chance of him graduating from the Academy as a full lieutenant.
With the best of luck, he could only make junior lieutenant. We
looked forward to the day when we would graduate and take our
revenge. But alas! During the final state exams, Stulov disappeared
from our platoon as suddenly as he had arrived . . .

All kinds of amateur musical and theatrical activities provided an
escape from the routine of the Academy. I was among those who
volunteered for the Academy choir (members were excused extra
labour duties, such as, for example, rescuing bags of tobacco from
the flooded River Tom'). During the audition, I tried to sing the
words of the song as loud as possible, without listening too much
to the melody, played on a piano. My ear failed me and I was not
accepted: yet it seemed to me that other cadets – who had quieter
voices – were welcomed in.

We were also taken to the cinema, which was located in a large
building next to our barracks. We gladly went in order to catch up
on some sleep. No one would notice us sleeping in the darkness. We
were constantly short of sleep. But sleeping before 'Retreat' was
forbidden. We had ten hours of classes and tactical training, mostly
outdoors in the extreme cold, and four hours of homework under
the surveillance of an officer. The rest of the time was consumed by
catering, washing, and so on. We did not have any time for personal
business.

During the winter, we also had cross-country skiing races on the
frozen Tom' river. We had to demonstrate both speed and stamina
in these races. All the cadets of the Academy took part. The Tom'
was covered with thick ice and had a sufficient layer of snow on it.
There were two good ski-tracks made for us. It was an easy task for
the Siberian cadets, as skiing was their natural means of winter
transportation. For us cadets from Leningrad, and especially for me,
this long race was hard and challenging. I fell behind the main group
from the very beginning. More and more cadets passed me by until
I was hopelessly separated from my group. What could I do? The
platoon leader would not be proud of me and all the boys would
laugh at me.

From the map, I knew the Tom' made a loop in this area. I did not have to think for long: but took off my skis, hoisted them on my shoulder, and climbed the steep bank of the frozen river. After descending onto the ice again, I saw that the ski-track was perfectly empty. I assumed I was still far behind the others, and began skiing as fast as I could. I was a little surprised, therefore, when a couple of skiers passed me once again, at the very end of the race: but imagine my astonishment when I learned I was the third to finish! Serbin, our platoon leader, praised me so much I had to tell him the truth – that I made a shortcut on foot – but he did not scold me, and began praising me once more, this time for my resourcefulness.

During a tactical training session we were ordered to build, equip, and camouflage a battery observation post in one night. The place for the post was on the slope of a hill, some 6 or 7 kilometres from the town. The frost was quite Siberian, about minus 40. We took all sorts of entrenching tools – pickaxes, spades, shovels – and as darkness fell, we began work. We removed a 1 metre layer of snow and started hacking into the frozen soil with pickaxes. When we reached soft, unfrozen soil, we were sweaty and exhausted. We fell down on this soft soil and rested for fifteen minutes. But within this short time, the soil began to freeze, and we had to take up our pick-axes again. We repeated this operation several times before the depth of the dugout reached about 2 metres. Then we sawed logs, planned the location of the observation post, built a roof for it and placed a field artillery periscope inside. At dawn we covered the roof with soil, fir branches, and snow. Exhausted but satisfied with the work we had done, we dropped to the floor of the post and fell asleep. But a bitter disappointment awaited us in the morning. Our battalion commander arrived and informed us our post had been spotted, and we had to build a new one in another place, with even stricter camouflage measures.

Eventually, examinations were upon us. If a cadet passed the main exam with an 'Excellent' grade and 'Good' in minor subjects, then he would be commissioned as a lieutenant. But if the grades were lower, he would graduate as a junior lieutenant. During my entire course of training I had achieved excellent grades in all subjects and was hoping to be commissioned as a lieutenant, but . . . my tooth failed me. Just before the exams I had an awful toothache, with a gumboil and fever. They put me in hospital, but I did not want to fall behind and spend six months more in the Academy, so I asked my superiors to let me do the exams anyway. They agreed, but the tooth failed me during drill exam. I could not march with a ceremonial step and give commands in a loud voice, as this jarred my tooth with hellish pain. The result? I only received 'Good' for the drill exam and was commissioned as a junior lieutenant. I was not too upset. I just wanted to leave the Academy as quickly as possible. As the officers' saying goes: 'You can't be sent further than the Front; you can't get less than a platoon to lead.'

In May 1943 we were issued new uniforms, map cases, pistol holsters, field shoulder boards with one stripe, and three books: uniform, food, and payroll. It was a great pleasure for us to attach the small stars to our shoulder boards: we were officers! Then they read out the postings: 60 per cent of officers were to go to Iran, 25 per cent to the Ural Artillery Training Centre, and only 15 per cent to the Front. I was in the latter 15 per cent.

There was no graduation ceremony or party. Freshly graduated, we eighteen-year-old officers had to go straight into battle. Our platoon leader, Lieutenant Serbin, escorted us to the Central Front. We boarded a cattle train, hastily equipped with bunk beds for the transportation of troops, and our journey began. Through the open sliding door of our truck we could see the Siberian landscape: the Taiga forests and the green spring steppe under a blue sky. Mighty twin FD steam engines pulled our train to the Front, belching out thick black smoke, which spread like a blanket over the woodland for miles around.

Fire Platoon Leader

Eighteen- and nineteen-year-old lieutenants came into the Red Army in 1943 after completing intensive training in different special schools and military academies. We were not afraid of going to the Front: we wanted to go into battle as quickly as possible, and if someone had told us that many of us would be killed in our very first action, we would not have believed them. A veteran of the Great Patriotic War, who also joined the Red Army as an eighteen-year-old lieutenant, later observed: 'this must be some sort of mystery of war. A person does not believe he could be killed. If he constantly thought about being killed, he would not be able to stand up and storm the enemy's positions; he would not be able to spend a single day at the Front.'

It was May 1943 when we arrived at the Central Front. We arrived in a small town – I don't remember its name. It was springtime, the sun was shining, and nothing – save the wrecked train station – reminded us of the war. Lieutenant Serbin gave us permission to walk around town a bit, while we waited for a truck. We were standing in the street – there were a few pedestrians walking about – when a priest in a black robe passed by, greeting us, 'Good day, Comrade officers!' We were amazed, but replied 'Good day!' One of us noticed an Order of the Red Banner on the priest's robe. We could not believe it. We ran after the cleric and yes, indeed, an Order of the Red Banner was pinned on his breast! We were shocked. A woman, who was passing, saw our amazement and explained to us that the priest had led a local partisan unit during the German occupation, but was now serving in the local church again.

When all our papers were processed, we left the town and went to a small village called Svoboda, which means 'Freedom'. In 1943 we did not know that the HQ of the Central Front was located in that village. Lieutenant Serbin handed over our papers, wished us luck in the war, said goodbye and left. Half an hour later we were all assigned to the 60th Army, under Lieutenant General Chernyakhovski, and hitch-hiked a truck to HQ. We were received by the chief of artillery. After a brief interview, I was assigned to the 497th Army Mortar Regiment together with four more officers. I tried to object, saying that we had not studied mortars, but the answer was: 'You are too young to decide where you will serve. You will fight this war in the unit where I send you. Your knowledge from the Academy is sufficient to be an officer in a mortar regiment!'

We arrived at the regiment late at night. From the stench of decomposing corpses and the sound of MG fire in the distance, we knew the Front was near. The regimental chief of staff received us, and – as it went at the Front – he asked us if there were any fellow-countrymen among us. As I was born in a village in the Tula area, it turned out he was from a neighbouring region. He distributed the other officers among various batteries and sent them away. When we were left alone, he offered me the post of deputy chief of staff (intelligence). It was a very responsible position, and in those days should have been filled by a captain, at the very least. I was a junior lieutenant, aged eighteen, and fresh out of the Academy! I was not only daunted by the complexity of a job for which I had no experience, but also by the huge responsibility of working in a regimental HQ during military operations.

The chief of staff made light of my fears: 'Take it easy, fellow-countryman, it will be all right. You are a graduate from an academy, while most of our officers here in the regiment are promoted NCOs and don't have any special artillery training.' But I bluntly refused, asking instead to be sent to a battery as a fire platoon leader. 'It's up to you, my friend. I wanted to give you a better spot, but if you are eager to work as a fire platoon leader, I'll send you to the best battery of the regiment – the 1st Battery, 1st Battalion.' He called a runner and ordered him to take me to the 1st Battery.

Our 497th Army Mortar Regiment was stationed on the River Seim, at the westernmost point of the Kursk salient, right opposite Rylsk city. During the night, the runner took me to the 1st Battery through an elaborate network of communication trenches. I stepped into the dugout of the battery commander and reported to him. After a brief conversation, including the traditional question as to whether or not I was a fellow-countryman, the battery commander ordered dinner and poured vodka into an aluminum cup, raising a welcoming toast to me. When I told him I did not drink, he replied: 'Everyone drinks at the Front! You should forget being a Mummy's boy and be a real man.' I drank the vodka, ate the food, and then went into my new dugout, where I fell fast asleep.

The runner woke me up next day around noon and told me to report to the battery commander. This I did, after washing, but I was simply ordered to have breakfast and then take over my platoon. As I had never seen mortars in real life (we only saw pictures in textbooks at the Academy), I asked the battery commander if I could first study the firing manual before taking over my platoon. He replied that he did not have any manuals, or any other documents, except for tables of sights. In his opinion, a table of sights was quite sufficient for leading the fire missions of a platoon. He repeated his order to take over the platoon and re-commended me to study the hardware and rules of firing in action.

After breakfast, the battery commander introduced me to the 3rd Platoon, which was lined up at the firing positions. He commanded the men to welcome me, take good care of me, and left. I greeted the platoon, and after getting to know the names of all the men, I ordered: 'Dismissed! gun leaders, assemble on me!'

The men in the platoon were experienced and battle-hardened, between twenty-five and forty-five years old. I knew I had to win their respect from the first day: I simply could not demonstrate my lack of knowledge regarding hardware, especially mortars. I also had to demonstrate that I was a demanding and strict officer. When I was alone with the gun leaders, I ordered them to show me their mortars. The mortars were standing in trenches about 170 centi-metres deep, built according to regulations, and thoroughly camouflaged (commanders on the Kursk salient were especially strict about camouflage – firing positions, communication trenches, dugouts, were all concealed – and the turf we used had to be kept fresh and green all the time). The gun leaders gave distinct and clear answers to my totally improvised 'hardware exam'. The names of the mortar parts were strange and completely new to me: 'tube', 'bipod carriage', 'support plate', and so on. However, after I checked and cross-checked the answers, I realized their answers were correct. For good measure, I chastised one gun leader, pointing out that the handles on the plate of mortar No. 6 were covered with rust. Then I let them go, and went to introduce myself to the other officers of the battery.

The lieutenants of the 1st and 2nd Platoons had learned everything from practice: they were all ex-NCOs. They received me well, sharing tables of fire for the mortars, and confirming that my sergeants had given correct answers during my impromptu 'exam'.

Who Fired at the Fritz?

The 120 millimetre regimental mortars could operate with the firing pin fixed on both 'hard' and 'soft'. In the former case, shells would be kicked out of the tube immediately after being loaded, in the latter case, shells would be fired when a rope was pulled. A shell weighing 15.9 kilogram and could fly as far as 5.7 kilometres. Shell fuses could be set for fragmentation (explosion on contact) or high-explosive (a delayed explosion, suitable for use against fortifications). A mortar battery could fire salvoes, in accordance with the artillery theory I knew from the Academy. The only thing the mortars could not do was fire directly at the enemy's tanks: consequently, each crew had an anti-tank rifle for defence against enemy armour.

But there was not much action in our area: mostly exchanges of fire between artillery and mortar batteries plus air strikes. The Fritzes were quiet. They fired illumination flares at night and maintained harassing fire with artillery and mortars, forcing us to use the trench network and avoid walking in the open. During the day, they put an artillery observation plane high in the sky. It was a twin-fuselage Focke-Wulf 189, which we dubbed a *Rama* ['Frame' – editor's note], due to its distinctive shape. Apparently, it had an armoured fuselage, as it was extremely hard to shoot down.

I quickly learned the ropes of a platoon leader, and two weeks after my arrival at the Front I was carrying out firing missions at night from a 'roving mortar'. We used this tactic in order not to give away our main firing positions. One mortar crew would creep away from the main firing position to fire at German MG nests that had been spotted during the day. We fired from various spots, quickly changing position afterwards. In the morning, the Germans would fire at the places where our mortars had been: but we were no longer there! In order to confuse the Fritzes even more, we often left a dummy mortar – or a whole dummy battery – made of wood at the spot from which a roving mortar had fired. The result was beyond our expectations. The German Air Force and artillery expended a lot of effort destroying these dummy mortar nests, while we sat in our trenches in peace. We decided to use this trick every time we fired from a roving mortar and it always worked. The only problem was finding new logs, as the dummy battery would be completely destroyed after a German bombardment. Very few shells landed on our main positions: those that did were sent over during harassing fire.

One day we saw a German *Rama* flying low from the direction of Kursk. There was an infantry unit stationed next to us. A soldier grabbed his rifle and opened fire on the *Rama*. After several shots, the plane started spinning in the air and fell down at the forward positions of our infantry and observation post. Probably it had been damaged before the soldier fired on it, but the fact is that it fell down after the infantryman fired. I saw officers running towards our positions, shouting: 'Who fired at the *Rama*? Who fired at the Fritz? Who fired at the German plane?' We pointed out the infantryman to them. The infantryman was scared, waiting to be scolded by the officers. But on the contrary, they congratulated him and told him he would be awarded with the Order of the Red Banner for bringing down the plane. I decided we should also try to get some decorations in this way, as we had bags of firepower, including six 14.5 millimetre anti-tank rifles. We set these on the wheels of old carriages and fired salvoes at any German plane we saw. But all our attempts were in vain, and we failed to down a single Fritz!

Typhus

In late June, I was sent to Army HQ with a report. While walking through a village, I decided to ask for directions and wandered into a peasant's hut. The hut was empty. When I asked: 'Is there anyone here?' a peasant woman's head popped out from a Russian stove! The woman said she was taking a steam bath inside the stove! I made a quick exit and asked for directions from some pedestrians on the street . . .

After I came back from Army HQ I felt sick. I felt cold and my whole body was shivering. Despite the hot summer weather, I could not get warm. My orderly made a stove in our dugout but I was still shivering. In the evening I passed out. They took me to a hospital during the night, and I was diagnosis with typhus. This was an emergency situation for the whole Army. The military doctors could not understand where the virus had could come from: all our troops were in static defence and all personnel were regularly examined and washed in mobile steam baths every week. I got the virus when I walked into that hut to ask for directions!

The disease hit me in its heavy form: a fever of around 40 degrees Celsius. I frequently passed out and became delirious. In short, it was a nightmare. Eventually the crisis passed, the fever disappeared, my appetite returned. The resilience of my young body – and the efforts of the doctors – meant I soon started to get better. Within two weeks of my recovery I was able to walk, but somewhat unsteadily. In fact, I was so weak that when I walked down to the River Seim, I could not climb back up the steep bank, and the medics had to fetch me back to the hospital. When I regained strength, I asked the doctors for permission to return to my battery: my wish was granted, but I was relieved from any physical work at the battery for two weeks.

A Useless and Bloody Assault

The nights of early August 1943 were warm and quiet. The Fritzes would bring up a loudspeaker mounted on a truck and give propaganda speeches. They used Russian traitors and defectors for this purpose. Often we would hear: 'I am a simple Russian peasant from the Kursk area, I defected to the Germans. They give us free land here, come here to the German side!' Etc., etc. We could hear these speeches very well, even though our positions were 2 kilometres behind the front line. When I heard such speeches, I would call Lieutenant Zezev at the battery observation post. We did not have a loudspeaker, but we had a gramophone, and I would tell Zezev to convey our common opinion about the Germans through the gramophone pipe: adding the worst curses at the end. A long and intensive artillery and machine-gun firefight would erupt after such exchanges of 'opinion'.

In the second week of August 1943, our battery received a huge amount of ammunition. New infantry units arrived at our positions. A regimental artillery battery consisting of ZIS-3 76.2 millimetre guns arrived and set up their positions to the left from us. We received an order to prepare for firing at all targets that had been spotted during the long months of static warfare. We were to open up from the main firing positions: it was our turn now! We fired as fast and as furiously as we could. The entire battery was firing on the first German trench, as well as their rear positions on the other side of the River Seim.

But I was puzzled that it was only our battery firing at the Germans, and not the entire regiment. The Germans had been building their defences for more than three months, and it would take a massive artillery and air strike from all available units to destroy them. Yet there was no such strike delivered from our side. After we had fired on the German weapon emplacements, we were ordered to drop our shells into the enemy's rear. Then our infantry launched an assault. The barrels of our mortars were red-hot from rapid firing. But despite this intense barrage, the German defences remained intact and our infantry suffered heavy casualties when crossing the river. Crowds of wounded walked back to our positions, on their way to the rear. They told us the Seim was red with blood. This murderous affair lasted all the way into the evening. I was puzzled at the action of our commanders: why had they ordered such a useless and bloody assault? It was only later I read that this whole operation had been a mere feint, a ruse, or distracting manoeuvre.

Fire Mission Over

In the evening we received an unexpected order: 'Fire mission over! Prepare for night march!' We were only given three hours to prepare for this march – not nearly enough time, considering we had been in position for three months. We were very well settled where we were! All mortar crews had well-built dugouts with three layers of logs on top. The walls and roofs of the dugouts were covered with *plash-palatkas* (waterproof rain capes). Inside, the beds were covered with fresh hay and also lined with rain capes. There were lamps on the tables, made from artillery cartridges. We officers had similar dugouts: the difference being we had real mattresses on our beds – God only knows where the sergeant major got them from! As for the firing positions of the mortars, they were built in full accordance with the fortification manuals: the foxhole for the mortar was the same length as the mortar's barrel, and the walls were lined with wooden desks. All dugouts and firing positions were connected by a system of trenches. The breastworks of the trenches were carefully camouflaged with fresh turf, and the shelters for mortar crews – having been dug in orchards – were well-camouflaged by the branches of the apple trees. The service units of the regiment – kitchen, steam bath, and other facilities – remained behind the firing positions. There were food warehouses, ammunition depots, shelters for mortar carriages, horses, and so on. We even had our own cow in the regiment, which was taken care of by a medic girl. Cow's milk normally went to the sick – or to whoever got there first! And so it was not an easy thing to leave all these comforts behind and march off. But despite all difficulties, we completed our preparations and made it within the three hours. Of course, we had to leave some bulky items behind. We made a gift of the cow to the local villagers.

We marched through a dark, still night. It felt good to be active again, after a long period of idleness in defence, and we made our first break in the morning.

I was summoned to the battalion's HQ. It turned out the Battery's Party Commission (BPC) held a session there. I had been called as a possible candidate for the Communist Party. I did not know anyone in the commission, except the battery's political officer, who had recommended me. They read out my application, listened to my brief biography, and began asking questions. The first question was: 'have you been in action?' I answered, that I had not been. The members of the commission were amazed by my answer, and the political officer of the battery inquired: 'Did you fire at the enemy with your fire platoon and battery?' 'Yes, I did!' 'And did enemy return fire?' 'Why, yes!' 'So why do you tell us that you have not been in action?' I replied that I thought they were speaking about hand-to-hand fighting, or firing from an open position in direct contact with enemy. The members of the commission had to hide their smiles and voted for me to become a candidate for the Communist Party of the Soviet Union (in those days it was still called the All-Russian Communist Bolshevik Party).

After the session was over, the deputy battery commander congratulated me on becoming a successful candidate. On the way back to the battery, he told me our battery commander was about to be transferred to another battalion and I would replace him soon. This news was as good as it was unexpected, especially as my relations with the battery commander were fairly frosty.

I was a an eighteen-year-old junior lieutenant, I had been at the Front barely three months, and now I was to take over a battery that contained many officers much more experienced than me! But the news was also worrisome: for I would be responsible not only for the battle performance of the battery, but also for all supply and administrative tasks. I shared these concerns with the deputy battery commander. He calmed me down, saying all those things could be taken care of – the papers promoting me to lieutenant were ready – but not to tell the battery commander about this.

The rest of the day was occupied with a difficult march under a hot August sun. The horses could barely pull the overloaded carriages, the wheels of which constantly sank in sand. The drivers trudged next to the carriages, pushing them when the going was tough, helping their exhausted horses as much as they could. Despite having only a map case to carry, I, too, was exhausted by our march through the sand. I wanted to ride on a carriage, but I banished this thought from my mind, and continued to tramp with my battery in the dust and heat, through a steppe that seemed endless. We were moving to a concentration area in order to deliver a strike on German forces in the area of Sevsk.

It grew cooler in the evening and we marched on a hard road: men and horses cheered up, foretasting the night rest. Soon after midnight, during the first hours of 16 August 1943, our battalion stopped in a large garden. The battalion commander ordered us to dig in and indicated the places for firing positions. As a senior officer of the battery, I pointed out sectors to the gun leaders, who, in their turn, marked the places for future firing positions, and the crews began digging in.

The order for me to take over the battery came that night and I was ordered to the observation post to prepare data for a joint fire mission involving the battery and its forward observation platoon. They were still building the observation post and laying phone cables between different spots, so I decided to take a nap. I dropped on the ground and fell asleep immediately.

I was woken by explosions nearby, followed by a sharp smack on the legs, as if an invisible hand had swiped me with a stick. There was a strong smell of blood – pungent, unfamiliar. Instinctively, I leaped up and dived into the nearest foxhole. The Fritzes were pouring in fire from regimental mortars, pounding away at the concentrated mass of our troops (unlike a grenade, a mortar shell hits everything above ground, so lying flat won't help). I had not yet understood I was wounded and anxiously looked around: enemy shells had hit five men from our battery, who were being bandaged; the leader of the 2nd Platoon was bandaging another wounded man and asked me for help. I tried to jump to my feet but it was in vain: my left leg no longer seemed part of my body! I could not move it. Blood was seeping through my uniform. I touched my legs and saw my hands were dripping in blood. Both legs were wounded. I told the lieutenant I had been hit myself.

They quickly bandaged me. They had to cut my long boot open as it was swollen with blood and impossible to take off. They put bandages over my trousers. I could no longer walk and they put me on a cart with the rest of the wounded. I told the platoon leader to take me over to the battery, said goodbye to all the men, and ordered the driver to take us to a field hospital. That was the last time I saw anyone from the 497th Army Mortar Regiment.

A Souvenir

We drove quickly but carefully, bypassing large holes and stones on the road. Nevertheless, I felt a searing pain in my left leg from even the smallest movement. We arrived at the medical battalion the same night. They gave us a tetanus vaccination, put us on beds of straw, and prepared us for surgery.

The operating theatre was in a large tarpaulin tent, well illuminated with carbide lamps. There were several tables in the tent with wounded soldiers lying on them, nurses running around. They undressed me, cut my trousers open, and put me face down on a cold surgery table. Next to me, on a similar table, another wounded man was lying. There was not a spot on his body that had not been hit: he looked like one big piece of bloody flesh. The man was lying quietly, without making a sound, apparently unconscious. How did he manage to get hit by so many small splinters in his back? The doctors had already removed them and were preparing to bandage him.

The nurses preparing me for the operation were chatting about their surgeon: 'How can he be without sleep for three days and nights and still perform surgeries? He is about to collapse!' Now this news did not make me happy at all! But I had nothing left to do but lie there and wait for the surgeon to cut my flesh and get that damn splinter out of my left leg. They gave me several anaesthetic injections: I cannot say how many as I only felt pain from the first two.

The surgeon came and started to cut my flesh. I could hear the sound of my flesh being cut. The nurse, who was assisting, did not wipe away all the blood from the wound: consequently, a little cold stream ran under my stomach and made a small pool.

The surgeon made a wide, deep cut, and then tried to get the splinter out with all sorts of instruments. But nothing worked. Apparently, the splinter had entered my leg, journeyed almost all the way through – taking dirt and pieces of fabric with it – and stopped 2 centimetres short of exiting on the opposite side. It would, of course, have been much easier to extract the splinter from the other side: but then all the bits of debris and shredded uniform would remain in the wound, causing infection. The surgeon was right to pull the splinter out through the entry hole. He cut deeper. The anaesthetic wore off. Pain shot through me – so strong I had to summon all my willpower not to scream. The surgeon tried to calm me down: 'Take it easy, my friend, I am about to get it out, I need just a bit more time . . .'

I think he pulled the splinter out with his fingers, after putting his entire hand into the wound. He showed the splinter to me, put it into a piece of bandage, and gave it to me as a souvenir. It was heavy, with sharp torn edges, some 2 or 3 centimetres long. The nurse cleaned up my wound, disinfected it, and put a lot of cotton into the hole, which measured 9 by 12 centimetres. After bandaging, they put me on a truck with other wounded men, and took us to an evacuation hospital (or it maybe it was still just a medical battalion). The hospital was located in the wooden houses of a village. I was put into one such hut. They put me on a real bed and gave me some food. I fell fast asleep after all the excitement, anxiety, and a sleepless night.

I woke up as they brought another wounded man into my room. I opened my eyes and saw it was a major of the Medical Corps. Little by little, we began a conversation and I heard his story. It turned out he was the surgeon who had operated on me! He recognized me as soon as I told him about my wound. The major told me that immediately after I had been evacuated from the medical battalion, it had been raided by German bombers. The surgery tent took a direct hit and many patients and medical workers were killed. The major himself had received a serious splinter wound in his stomach. According to his own estimate his hours were numbered. I tried to reassure him everything would be all right: he answered that, as a surgeon, he knew very well everything was not all right.

They sent me further to the rear later that evening. The wounded major was not transportable. They did not even put him in a bed.

As they were taking me away from the room, I thanked the major for the surgery once again, and wished him a speedy recovery. He smiled back bitterly, wished me all the best, and said his life was over. When they were putting me into the medical truck, the nurse confirmed the sad truth that the wounded major would not live to see another day.

Lucky

I arrived at yet another hospital – or maybe again it was another medical battalion. It was a large barrack with two-level bunk beds arranged in three rows. They put me on a lower level. Despite the fact it was a large barrack with many wounded men inside, it was quiet and orderly. Nurses took care of the wounded, even rolling cigarettes for those whose hands were bandaged. Smoking was allowed, but not for all wounded at the same time, so the barrack was kept well ventilated and the air inside was fairly fresh. After more vaccinations I fell asleep again. But I was disturbed by loud voices and lively conversation in the barrack. They were putting someone next to me and the patients nearby were shouting: 'the lieutenant got lucky, there is a beautiful young girl lying next to him!' After some effort I managed to turn and felt something hard next to me: it was a female medic, a lieutenant, and her entire body was covered in plaster. Only her face remained visible. The girl was unconscious, but her face moved from time to time in pain. Who she was, and what had happened to her I never found out, as in the morning I was again put on a truck and taken to a railway station. They put us on a train – a proper passenger train with beds and all conveniences – and I again fell asleep (I should say I always slept some three days after being wounded, as I could not get enough sleep during battles and marches).

I was woken up by thunderous explosions: German planes were bombing the station. Through the window I could see fire and smoke. Our train was standing at a large station. A few tracks from us there was a burning medical train full of wounded. Medics were pulling wounded men out of the burning train and piling them on the platform nearby (a similar scene was depicted by a painter after the war – a rather realistic painting, it is exhibited in the Medical Corps Museum in Leningrad).

Our train pulled out. Nurses and medics started running around, preparing us for evacuation. They told us we were about to be removed and placed in a real, stationary, hospital. The train stopped several minutes later and they started to transfer us into ambulances. We drove through a city – the city of Kursk.

At last, we were put into a hospital attached to our Front. The building must have been a regular city hospital before the war. Before putting us into beds, we were washed and our bandages were changed. Our clothes were also changed for clean hospital robes. I was put into an officers' room on the second floor, which contained four beds: in one, a senior lieutenant was groaning from the pain in his injured leg; in another was a wounded major; the last bed was vacant. After a good dinner, I just wanted to fall asleep in my nice clean cot. But it was easier said than done: all of a sudden, the city's AA-guns opened fire and I heard the distant booming of bomb-blasts. 'Yet another air raid on the city: it's the same every night!' said the nurse on duty. Those wounded that could walk shuffled into a shelter. But we – the immobilized wounded – had to stay in our beds and not give in to panic. What else could we do? When the raid was over, and the bombers had flown away, all was quiet again. Only the grumbling of the wounded and the groans of the senior lieutenant could be heard . . .

In the morning, the chief surgeon of the hospital, escorted by other personnel, made an inspection of all the wounded. Our doctor would report on the type of wound and the condition of the wounded person. The chief surgeon would inspect the wounded person, ask if he had any complaints regarding the hospital, and then give orders to the doctors. He stopped at the bed of the senior lieutenant for a long time, inspecting his wound, and announcing an urgent amputation was necessary, as gangrene was spreading quickly. The surgery had to be performed immediately, the chief surgeon said: tomorrow would be too late. The senior lieutenant started shouting that he would not allow his leg to be amputated; that he would only be half a man without a leg; that his leg would be fine without doctors, and that all doctors should go to hell and leave him alone. But the chief surgeon breezed over to me and the major, then the entire group left the room.

During the inspection I complained about my leg: after surgery it had remained bent at an angle of 90 degrees and I could not straighten it. This was not only very uncomfortable – especially when using crutches – but my old rheumatism also made my knee very sore. Normally, I would relieve rheumatic pain by moving my leg about, but now this seemed impossible, and I had to ask a nurse to massage my knee. The chief surgeon told me I should try to straighten my leg every day, despite any pain, and then it would return to normal.

After the medical 'top brass' left, the major and I tried to convince the senior lieutenant to agree to amputation. We told him the chief surgeon was not joking about it, and one could live even without a leg. He responded with curses and a request to leave him alone as it was his own business. As to me, he added that I was too young to lecture him. When lunch arrived the senior lieutenant refused to eat, and told the nurse who tried to feed him to go to hell.

The Germans bombed the city again. The nurse told us they were going for the railway station again, with its large concentration of military trains. But bombs were also exploding next to our building so that it was shaking and shivering.

We all fell fast asleep after the air raid. When I woke up in the morning I realized the senior lieutenant was quiet and his groans could no longer be heard. When I turned in his direction, I saw that his body was covered with a white sheet. Medics quickly came and put the body of the senior lieutenant on a stretcher and left. The prediction of the chief surgeon had come true earlier than we had expected.

This is a Battle Mission Too,
By the Way

Next day, the inspection by the chief surgeon was repeated. He did not like the look of my leg, and told me my fate could be the same as that of the late senior lieutenant. Gangrene, he said, was a deadly disease that could be spotted in its early stages but not cured. At least not here: for he added that some clinics in Moscow had apparently found a successful treatment for it. I replied that I did not want to lose my legs or die so young – as had happened with the senior lieutenant – so a transfer to a Moscow clinic would be highly appreciated. The chief surgeon thought for a while, then ordered a doctor to prepare me for transfer to Moscow.

Within half an hour, an ambulance took me to an airfield. When we arrived, I saw a Douglas ambulance plane taking off. There were no more large planes on the field – it was empty. They took me to a tent and the ambulance drove away. There were three more wounded officers in the tent. The Douglas that had just flown away could not take them as it was already overloaded. The commander of the airfield arrived and started to ask himself aloud what he should do with us. We answered that we should be sent to Moscow as soon as possible as we all had serious wounds. 'I know that! If you had light wounds you would not have been here.' he replied. He added that he had two light U-2 *kukuruznik* biplanes on the airfield but they were under the direct command of Front Commander Rokossovski. The airfield commander said that if the Front HQ gave the go-ahead for using the U-2 planes, we could fly to Moscow in them. He returned in fifteen minutes and informed us permission had been obtained, and we were to be loaded onto the planes immediately. Each plane could carry an additional three persons besides the pilot: two sitting in the second cabin behind the pilot, and one lying in the fuselage. They put me in the second cabin with a wounded captain, who sat in front, facing me. There was very little space in the cabin. They secured us with seatbelts, wished us a safe flight, and closed the windows on either side of the cabin. The cabin had a perfect view: I did not even have to stick my head out in order to see the landscape. The engines roared, we took off effortlessly, and gradually gained altitude – though I could still see villages, forests, fields, and even individual people and cattle in the fields.

That was my first time in a plane and everything was new and unusual for me. The engine was rattling like a tractor in a field right next to me and it was hard to get used to it. The plane was constantly changing altitude, sometimes soaring higher and sometimes falling into air pits, so that my heart jumped up to my throat. The captain sitting in front of me went very pale: apparently, he was about to throw up. I did not feel any better than him.

In an hour or so the plane descended and softly landed on a large field in the middle of an apple orchard. The pilots opened our cabins and disappeared somewhere. We breathed the scent of the apple trees, enjoying the sudden silence. Our pilots came back soon, carrying large bags of apples behind their backs. They put the bags in the back of their planes, at the feet of the wounded men lying in the fuselage. Workers from the orchard *sovkhoz* [state-owned agricultural land – editor's note] also came along and brought us gifts – a bag packed full of big apples! They put them in the cabins at our feet.

I noticed all the pilots had several decorations. In those days – back in 1943 – it was still quite rare to see an officer with several decorations. I asked the them: 'What did you get all those orders for?' 'For battle missions, of course!' 'Did you fly to bomb Berlin or what?!' 'Well, we get our decorations for a certain number of battle missions. This is a battle mission too, by the way.' 'How come?' 'We are flying along the front line: German Messerschmitt fighters can attack us any time.'

The news of a possible German fighter attack did not make us any happier. However, this was war and all we could do was hope for the best. Our pilots told us they had been under fighter attack several times but were saved by the fact the U-2 could fly very low and was very manoeuvreable. It could even land in the middle of a corn field, hence the nickname: *kukuruznik*, a 'corn plane'. The pilots asked after our health, started their engines, and we took off again. We made a circle above the field, where workers of the *sovkhoz* were standing and waving at us, and continued our flight towards Moscow.

The flight lasted about six hours and we were quite exhausted after it: wounds and loss of blood – as well as our impracticality in the air – all did their job. In the evening, we saw the River Moscow below us. The pilots switched off their engines and we landed softly on Tushino Airfield. There was a large hospital tent right there on the field and they took us there. We were met by a nurse who was amazed to hear we had flown in on 'corn planes'. We told her we had been unlucky enough to miss the regular Douglas ambulance plane to Moscow. The nurse replied: 'Is that the Douglas plane that crashed, shot down by the Germans? It must have been! No Douglas plane landed here today!'

Late in the evening we finally arrived at a large hospital, located in the buildings and dormitories of the Timiryazev Academy. After some formalities, they put us all into different rooms. I still had the bag of apples with me, and I was happy to share them with the nurses and my fellow-wounded. One nurse, at first, refused to take a single apple from me. According to her, such apples cost around 25 roubles each in Moscow. But finally she took one, and I gave all the apples away to wounded men and nurses, leaving only three for myself.

The Visiting Artists from Aleksin

During an inspection, my new surgeon said I would not get gangrene, and in order to be 100 per cent sure, they made several small cuts and injections around the wound (I suspect it was penicillin). I did not stay in that hospital for long, but was transferred to yet another stationary hospital in Moscow. It was a hospital that had state-of-the-art equipment and everything was designed and arranged for the fastest healing. I remember that the hospital was located next to a large aircraft factory, as we could hear its noise from the windows of our rooms.

Here, from the windows of our hospital, we watched a salute celebrating the liberation of Kiev. By the order of the commander-in-chief, our 497th Army Mortar Regiment was awarded the honorary title of 'Kiev'.

There was a nice living room next to our ward. It had soft sofas and chairs. For us *frontoviks*, this was not a hospital, but heaven on earth! The medical personnel of the hospital – from the chief surgeon to the simplest nurse – treated us the best way they could and were very friendly. Of course, in such conditions, I started to court a young nurse. She was happy with it, and other wounded officers – mostly older than me – tried to assist us in every manner, warning us when the duty officer or senior nurse was coming! My wounds were gradually healing: I could already walk without crutches. Doctors started talking about transferring me to a recovery hospital. And soon they did. In mid-November 1943 I was transferred to Aleksin Sanatorium in Sokolnitski Park. This sanatorium housed an officer recovery hospital. The room where I stayed was the former club room of the sanatorium. In fact, beds stood both in the former hall and on the former stage. There were over sixty men staying in that hall. The hospital had one common canteen where all the wounded would eat.

In the mornings, they would read out the orders of the hospital regarding disciplinary measures against officers who had broken the house rules – i.e. those officers who had gone absent without leave and had been caught in Moscow by the military police. The orders also included punishments, in the form of house arrests for several days, to be served in the units where the offending officers came from. For us *frontoviks* this was a pure formality, except for the fact they withheld 50 per cent of our wages for the days of house arrests.

As we did not have any military uniforms – our clothing consisted of a hospital robe with underwear sticking out of it and slippers – we were only permitted to walk in the yard of the sanatorium, which was surrounded by a fence. If the weather was fine we were also allowed to walk in the park.

My eyesight was not too good – I was longsighted. Even when I had to go through the medical examination before entering the special artillery school in Leningrad, I sent my friend Sergei Zorin, who had good eyesight, to the eye doctor instead of me. I needed eyeglasses, so I spoke to my doctor and he sent me to a garrison hospital in Moscow that had an eye doctor. I received all the necessary papers plus a uniform, and after visiting the garrison hospital I had a chance of spending some time in Moscow. I went straight back to my previous hospital and invited my girlfriend nurse to come to the city with me. She managed to get several hours' leave from the senior nurse and we had a great time in Moscow, even making it to a cinema not far from Red Square. My girlfriend was a student, and just like me, she was eighteen years old. We were young, and despite the war, we had a good time dreaming about a beautiful, happy future.

Moscow looked strict and stern in 1943. Red Square seemed quite small to me – probably because there were dummy building roofs painted on the pavement, in order to deceive German bombers. Even dummy building silhouettes were painted on the Kremlin walls. But I was most impressed with Moscow's metro: Leningrad did not have such an underground system. In fact, in those days, only Moscow had a metro in the entire Soviet Union. Compared to the strict-looking streets of wartime Moscow, the metro stations looked like luxurious underground palaces.

I also went to see the eye doctor in the garrison hospital and he ordered my glasses. However, I did not use these glasses for long, as during Operation Bagration the map case where I kept them was torn into pieces by a German shell. Luckily, I was not in the trench where I had left my map case when it got hit!

When other recovering officers heard I had been given a uniform, they asked me to hang on to it for as long as possible, and borrowed it from me in order to slip away to the city. We took turns using it until I was finally forced to return it to the hospital some six days later. Sometimes I would borrow uniforms from other officers, who had also been issued them for temporary use.

One time, I was caught by the military police next to a metro station in Moscow, wearing someone else's uniform. As I did not have any papers with me, I was taken to the commandant's office. Since the commandant knew about the adventures of recovering officers from our hospital, he dubbed us, 'the visiting artists from Aleksin'.

After a brief interrogation, all the officers that had been detained were lined in the corridor of the commandant's house. The deputy commandant ordered: 'Officers serving in line, one step forward!' No one moved (I was also standing still as my wound had not yet completely healed). The rest of the officers were from supply units – hospitals etc. – and had been detained for breaking uniform regulations, failing to salute to superior officers in the street, or other minor military wrongdoings.

The deputy commandant stopped in front of me and ordered me to step out. The command delivered to the remaining malefactors was short: 'Perform two hours of drill in front of the commandant's house and then everyone is released!' I was freed without punishment, while the other officers received three days' house arrest for good measure.

Frontoviks

My wounds finally healed and on 21 November. I was ordered to transfer to a reserve officer artillery regiment in Narofominsk. I was permitted to report to the regiment within five days, as I had been given five days' worth of leave and dry tack upon my discharge from the hospital. Leningrad was still under siege – I had nowhere to go – so I went directly to the regiment in Narofominsk. I reported to the regiment the same day and turned in all my papers. I was sent to an artillery battalion that was stationed in a large barrack built for some 100 men. There were no free beds! In fact, there were two officers sleeping on each bed, so I was invited to spend the night on a window sill: it was wide enough, but cold as ice, as it was made of concrete and there was a draught coming from the window.

The officers in the battalion performed guard duty, took turns as duty officers, washed floors: in short, they did all the soldiers' jobs. They immediately wanted to make me wash a floor, but I showed them the papers stating I was still on leave, and they left me alone. I did not have any breakfast that day and arrived too late for lunch. Perhaps I would not have received food anyway, as my papers had not yet been processed. So I took my dry tack and went into the city, hoping to find somewhere to prepare something edible from it.

I went to the nearest house in the village – actually part of the small town of Narofominsk – and knocked on the door. A woman in uniform, with the rank of sergeant, opened the door and asked me what I wanted. I said I wanted to see the landlady. She smiled and went into the house. Another woman appeared, this time a senior lieutenant, and said she was the landlady. I apologized and wanted to leave, but she asked me why I needed to see her. When she realized I only wanted to make some food from my dry tack, she said she was about to have dinner and would be pleased if I could join them. It would have been impolite to refuse so I stepped into the house.

There were three more officers and two sergeants in the house, all girls. They addressed each other by first names, without using military ranks. They were very polite and asked a lot of questions about me: who was I? Where was I from? And so on. As the conversation progressed, I learned that the girls were from a special sub-machine gun regiment stationed in the village. Many of the girls had already been at the Front and had decorations. The landlady, or senior lieutenant, invited me to visit them again and maybe even stay overnight. I thanked them and returned to my regiment.

There were all sorts of persons in the regiment: there were officers like me, sent to the reserve regiment after a wound and longing to go back to the Front; but there were also officers who tried to stay as far as possible from the Front. Here I met an officer who graduated from the same artillery academy as me. He was sent to the reserve regiment after graduation in 1942 and had not yet been at the Front at all! He spoke with some amusement about being sent on different duties here and there. In his opinion, life in the reserve regiment, with all its inconveniences – such as bad food – was better than life at the Front with all its dangers. People like him preferred to stay alive by cleaning toilets than risk death or injury by leading a battery in battle. But *frontoviks* did not stay in the regiment for long: they volunteered for front line service and were quickly sent back into action (especially as regimental representatives, coming to pick up officer replacements, were eager to have those who already had battle experience). I, too, wrote an immediate request to the battalion commander, asking to be sent back to the Front. He promised to send me away as soon as possible.

That night I slept badly. My window sill was quite a contrast to a soft hospital bed, being cold, hard, and draughty. I turned from side to side but could not get comfortable. Eventually, I fell into a half-sleep – lulled by a chorus of snoring officers – and dreamed about getting an order to go to a front line unit, going to Moscow for a couple of days to see my girlfriend, and then arriving at the Front. In the early morning I managed to doze off completely.

Cavalrymen of Kotovski,
Saddle Your Horses!

The second day of my stay in the reserve officer regiment did not bring any news. I wandered around Narofominsk all morning before returning for lunch at the regimental canteen. In the afternoon I had a nap on a free bed in the barrack. The evening was the same – dull and boring. When all the officers returned to barracks I went back to my window sill, as there were no more vacant beds. A duty officer woke me up at midnight, and ordered me to report immediately to battalion HQ. I put myself in order and went to the HQ, where I found seven more officers who had been summoned just like me. The duty officer read an order from the battalion commander, granting our requests for front line postings: we were to be sent to the III Guards Cavalry Corps. The officer added that we should be happy to fight the war in such a famous and prestigious unit.

I thought nothing could surprise me, having been sent to serve in a mortar unit after studying in an artillery school, but to be sent to the cavalry! I simply could not conceive it! 'Are there any questions?' Asked the representative of the III Guards Cavalry Corps, a lieutenant colonel, who snapped the spurs on his long boots as he spoke. Everyone was silent. I asked the lieutenant colonel if the corps had any artillery at all. He replied that the corps had artillery, tanks, *Katyusha* rocket-launchers, and even its own planes. Someone asked when we were due to leave for the corps. 'Immediately, our Studebaker trucks are waiting outside . . .'

Subsequent events unfolded with lightning speed. We were loaded onto the truck and several hours later we were at the corps' HQ, reporting to the chief of artillery. In a matter of minutes we were distributed between different divisions, and I was sent to the 5th Guards Cavalry Division. From the divisional HQ I was sent to the 24th Guards Cavalry Regiment. At the regimental HQ I was welcomed by V. F. Todchuk, a cultured Guards captain who embodied all the best features of a cavalry officer. With a friendly smile, he told me there were no vacancies for an artillery officer in the regiment, but as it was marching to the Front and was about to go into battle, they were sure to find a place for me. I was not too encouraged by this news, but Todchuk added: 'Don't lose heart, artillery expert. You are now in the famous Red Banner Guards Regiment, which is part of the even more famous Red Banner Order of Lenin Bessarabiya Kotovski Guards Division. For the moment you will stay with the regimental 76 millimetre battery, and we will see what we can do for you later.' [Although unusual to Western eyes, such a cumbersome designation for a Red Army unit was not unusual. All honorary titles and distinctions had to be cited together, and this could make a unit's official name a lengthy affair. It was also a matter of status: the longer the name, the more distinguished the unit. And so, although unofficially known as the 5th Guards Cavalry, the unit's full title in 1945 was the 5th Guards Red Banner Order of Lenin Order of Suvorov 2nd Degree Bessarabiya-Tannenberg Kotovski Cavalry Division – editor's note.]

He briefly told me the history of the division. It started as a cavalry brigade under Kotovski, a legendary Red Army commander of the Russian Civil War, and was later reformed into the 3rd Cavalry Division. The division fought from the very beginning of Great Patriotic War, taking part in the delaying battles of 1941, as well as making raids behind German lines. The division received an honorary Guards title for those battles and was renamed the 5th Guards Cavalry Division, while our regiment – previously the 158th Cavalry Regiment – became the 24th Guards Cavalry Regiment. Thus re-badged, the division took part in the Battle of Stalingrad. Most officers and men were decorated with the campaign medal: 'For the Defence of Stalingrad.' I was impressed with the origin, traditions, and titles of my new unit. Nevertheless, I thought cavalry

Ivan Yakushin's picture from his identification card, Central Front, 1943.
(From Ivan Yakushin collection)

Guards Lieutenant Yakushin with his wife Irina and son Alexander in 1950s, Leningrad.
(From Ivan Yakushin collection)

Officers and men of the 24th Guards Cavalry Regiment that distinguished themselves in Operation Bagration. Ivan Yakushin recalls: 'I and Zozulya walked up to the scene at the last moment, so we are both in the very last row. This picture is especially dear to me as this is the only picture of Guards Lieutenant Kuchmar that I have. He was killed in action on May 2 1945. He is standing immediately in front of me to the right. We are all still wearing regular Army headgear, *pilotka* garrison caps and visor caps. *Kubanka* hats were introduced in our Corps later.' *(From Ivan Yakushin collection)*

From right to left: AT-gun battery commander Agafonov, 1st AT-gun platoon leader Zozulya and 2nd AT-gun platoon leader Yakushin, 1945.

(From Ivan Yakushin collection)

...r Golovko performing stunts with his ...e, 1945. *(From Ivan Yakushin collection)*

Guards Sergeant Chernov on his horse.
(From Ivan Yakushin collection)

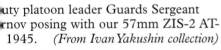

...uty platoon leader Guards Sergeant ...rnov posing with our 57mm ZIS-2 AT-...1945. *(From Ivan Yakushin collection)*

Guards Lieutenant Yakushin and Guards Private Balatski, 1945. Balatski is the soldier who lost his horse during a night march in 1944. *(From Ivan Yakushin collection)*

N.A. Lakov's dramatic 1945 painting *After an Enemy Air Raid on a Medic Train* which vividly captures the confusion and danger of the attack on the train that is recalled in the text. *(Courtesy of the Military Medical Museum, St Petersburg)*

A burnt-down Russian village, 1941. The wooden houses are burnt to ashes; only Russian stoves are intact. These stoves were so big that they were used for cooking and drying clothes and for taking steam baths, and people would sleep on top of them to keep warm in winter. *(From Bair Irincheev collection)*

AT-gun battery, 1945. *(From Ivan Yakushin collection)*

: our AT-gun battery commander Guards Senior Lieutenant Agafonov, 1945. Right:
ushin is sitting between two guards sergeants from the AT-gun battery. Both guards
eants are wearing parade uniforms as they both were given the top honour to represent
III Guards Cavalry Corps on the victory parade in Moscow on 24 June 1945. Both guard
eants are veterans of Battle of Stalingrad. *(Both from Ivan Yakushin collection)*

Official picture of Guards
Lieutenant Ivan Yakushin from
1945.
(From Ivan Yakushin collection)

Men of Yakushin's platoon drinking to celebrate victory, 9 May 1946.
(From Ivan Yakushin collection

Men of Yakushin's platoon dancing to accordion, 1945. *(From Ivan Yakushin collection)*

Men of Yakushin's platoon, Victory Day, 9 May 1946. *(From Ivan Yakushin collection)*

AT-gun platoon under Guards Lieutenant Yakushin, 1945.   *(From Ivan Yakushin collection*

AT-gun platoon under Guards Lieutenant Yakushin, 1945.   *(From Ivan Yakushin collection*

had no place in modern warfare and decided to leave the unit immediately after receiving my next wound. Later, however, my opinion radically changed, and I always returned to the cavalry after recovering from wounds.

After this meeting, the captain always referred to me as 'the artillery expert'. I still don't know why he called me that: there was probably a note in my papers, stating I had graduated from the Leningrad Special Artillery School and the Tomsk Artillery Academy. The captain called for a runner and ordered him to take me to the commander of the regimental artillery battery. He shook my hand, wished me luck, snapped his spurs, and walked away. The runner went to look for someone from the regimental battery, while I observed the daily life of a cavalry regiment: something that was completely new to me.

The regiment was on a day's rest and was hastily preparing for another march. Riders could be seen moving to and from HQ. Unlike infantry soldiers, cavalrymen were dressed in long boots, and their greatcoats had long slits up the back, so they could be worn in the saddle. Their shoulder boards had light blue piping, with the cavalry emblem – a horseshoe with two crossed sabres – in the middle. In addition to small arms, cavalrymen were armed with sabres. Despite disgusting November weather, the cavalrymen looked smart and fresh.

The runner came back a few minutes later and reported that the carriage of the battery's sergeant major had arrived at HQ, and the sergeant major would take me to the battery. The sergeant major was a tall and rather talkative cavalryman, who had started his service before the war. Mixing Russian and Ukrainian words, he asked me about myself all the way: where I was from, where I had lived, and where I had fought. When he heard I was a city boy and had never served in the cavalry, he explained that the most important element of the cavalry is the horse: the battle-companion of every cavalryman. The horse, he continued, is the Alpha and Omega – the beginning and the end of all things – for a cavalryman. No mission could be completed without it; and the main responsibility of both officers and men was to care for their mounts. A cavalryman, he concluded, must not fail his horse, and in this way, his horse would not fail in battle.

When we arrived at the battery, I found the battery commander and reported for duty as a reserve officer. The battery commander, a young officer some twenty-five years old, received me very well, and introduced me to the platoon leaders, with whom I immediately made friends and found common ground. Guards Lieutenant Kuchmar took special care of me, explaining the peculiarities of an artillery battery's role within a cavalry regiment. Smoking his pipe and smiling, he proposed I stayed in his platoon. I accepted the invitation with pleasure. The battery was stationed on the edge of a forest and was preparing for a night march. The battery had 76 millimetre field guns (Model 1939) as its main equipment; each piece was drawn by six good horses. The same gun in an infantry division would have been pulled by two horses only, but the difference is easily explained by the fact that the mounted batteries had to keep up with the sabre squadrons of the regiment.

The weather grew worse in the evening, and it started to rain. The drizzle was not strong but we saw it would last for ages. A cook arrived at his 'AA-gun' (this was the local nickname for a field kitchen) and started to dish out dinner. The dinner was put into canteens – two or three portions into each. Tea was poured in the same canteens after they were hastily washed. Kuchmar's driver brought dinner for us two officers in two canteens. He stretched a *plash-palatka* rain cape on the ground beneath a tree, set the canteens there, put out some bread, and offering me his own spoon (which he pulled out of his long boot), invited us to eat. Despite the rain, which was pouring into the collars of our greatcoats, into our meals, and into our tea, we all ate with a good appetite.

Before we could finish our food, a bugle sounded from the direction of the regimental HQ. 'Here it is – the order to saddle and mount,' said Kuchmar, as he stood up from the rain cape. It was quickly growing dark, but riders, officers, and drivers, calmly saddled their horses and prepared the carriages and guns for a night march. The 'saddling' signal was repeated several times, at different volumes: sometimes loud and brusque, sometimes melodic and sustained. 'Ca-val-ry-men, men of Ko-tov-ski, saddle your horses . . .' this was the signal that promised a long and difficult march.

The battery fell into line on the road and took its place in the column of the regiment. Darkness fell, and only the sound of tramping hooves gave away the presence of an entire corps. The rain continued all night without a break. Wheels and horseshoes combined with the deluge to reconstitute the surface of the road into a river of mud. Gun carriages sank up to their axles and floated, rather than rolled, through the slough. Despite the rain capes, which we wore on top of greatcoats, we were soaked to our skin. At dawn the temperature dropped, and instead of rain, biting flakes of ice fell from the sky, freezing our capes and greatcoats and transforming them into icy armour. The march was growing harder and we were all frozen to our bones. Men and horses impatiently waited for the signal to halt: no one even felt like smoking in such horrible weather. Finally, the long-desired bugle signal was given: 'Commanders' Gathering'. 'Commanders . . . commanders . . . gather, gather!' sounded the bugle, as the bugler rode along the column. The signal meant we would stop soon and have a chance to change clothes and dry our uniforms.

Here I should mention the two main bugle signals the Red Army cavalry used during the Great Patriotic War. The most common bugle signal was 'Saddle!' – a long melodic sound that woke up the riders and forced them to saddle horses and harness them into MG, gun, and ammunition carriages. The signal first sounded at the regimental HQ and was then repeated by all bugle players in the regiment: 'Ca-val-ry-men, men of Ko-tov-ski, saddle your horses . . .' That was its melody. The second signal was 'Commanders' Gathering.' This signal was more cheerful. It normally meant a break in the march would soon occur. It would usually sound some 5 kilometres from the rest area. Officers spurred on their horses and hurried up to the head of the column. 'Commanders, commanders . . . gather! gather!' sounded the signal. Sometimes the last part of the signal had an addition: 'concerns all commanders!'

Our battery was given a place for a day's rest next to two intact buildings of a village. As I did not yet have any responsibilities, Kuchmar suggested I went to have a rest in one of the houses. I was grateful to him for this, and went into the nearest house. Riders from the previous squadron were lying on the floor of the peasant hut like herrings in a can. It was warm, but the air was so thick, one could have hung a greatcoat in it. The heads of two children were sticking out from a bed atop the Russian stove. The kids were inspecting the sleeping soldiers with curiosity. A hospitable landlady advised me to take off my clothes and dry them next to the stove: 'You should also warm yourself – go and sleep on the stove next to my children while your clothes are drying.' I did not wait for another invitation, and avoiding the sleeping bodies, made it to the stove in two jumps. One cannot describe the bliss I experienced there, next to the warm stove: snug and cosy, I soon fell asleep.

My First Mistake in the Cavalry

One night, I was suddenly ordered to report to the regimental HQ. I carefully stepped over the sleeping bodies of my comrades, stretched out on the floor, and quietly left the hut. Outside it was snowing lightly and there were some snowdrifts. I reported to the regiment's deputy chief of staff, and he passed me an order from the regimental commander. The order read that I, Junior Lieutenant Yakushin, should immediately leave for divisional HQ, and remain at the disposal of the division's staff. I was ordered to get a horse from the regimental band and a saddle from the sapper platoon. These platoons were both located next to the regimental HQ. I awoke the sergeant major of the band platoon, and passed on the order to supply me with a horse. I did not know much about horses at this time, and asking the sergeant major to give me his best mount was my first mistake in the cavalry: for when he saw I had artillery shoulder boards with red piping (cavalrymen had light blue piping), he realized my ignorance and selected his meanest nag. He proceeded to praise the non-existent qualities of the poor creature, like a Gypsy horse trader, and succeeded in proving to me it really was the best beast in the stable.

I took the horse to the sapper platoon. They knew what I needed and the duty NCO offered me a selection of dragoon saddles. I pointed my finger at the first one I saw, and as I did not yet know how to saddle a horse, ordered him to do it for me. Then, as I had no clue how to mount a horse using stirrups, I left the stables and started looking for a suitable elevation from which I could lower myself onto my new steed. After several attempts, I dragged my horse into a ditch and mounted it. I was lucky this operation took place in complete darkness and that no one saw me: otherwise, my reputation in the regiment would have been lost for a long time – if not for good – and I would have become an eternal object of fun . . .

I rode a few dozen metres and then the horse stopped, refusing to take me any further. All my efforts to make the beast move were in vain. I had to dismount. It occurred to me the horse would not move because I had no spurs on my boots: so I tied it to a fence and went back to the battery on foot. When I arrived at our hut, I tried to rouse Kuchmar, in order to ask him for his spurs. But Kuchmar would not wake up and only mumbled when I shook him. Being afraid of disturbing the other men, I grabbed Kuchmar's long boots, removed the spurs, and put them on my own boots. This was my second mistake in the cavalry: for I put them on the wrong way, with the buckles on the inside.

I left the hut and walked towards my mount, making a whip from a tree branch, to be sure the nag would move. After mounting again – with great difficulty – I managed to make the horse trot towards divisional HQ. But the weather worsened, a blizzard blew up, and the road disappeared under a layer of snow. I did not notice, therefore, when we lost the road and tramped into a swamp. It became harder and harder for the horse to pull its feet out of the quagmire. The poor beast tried to reach solid ground with a big jump, but it did not have enough strength, and simply fell on its right side, taking me with it. I managed to pull my right leg free; then I stood up, helped the horse regain its legs, and led it out of the swamp. It was not an easy task. Only after we were both completely covered with muck, did I manage to get the nag onto solid ground. Luckily, the swamp was small and the blizzard had begun to grow weaker.

My horse was completely soaked after the adventure in the swamp: it was steaming. I, too, was drenched with sweat. But the blizzard stopped and I found the road. But time was ticking, and I had to ride on, in order to report to divisional HQ before dawn.

There were no ditches or hillocks on the road. It would have been completely stupid to walk with the horse, so I tried to mount it by putting my foot into a stirrup. I realized that if I mounted the horse from the right side I would be facing its tail, not its head: so I put my left foot into the left stirrup and after some difficulty, eventually succeeded in getting astride the animal. This was my first victory in horse riding exercises. On the way to HQ I dismounted and mounted the horse several times just for the sake of exercise.

After our joint mud bath the horse became very obedient and followed my commands even without a whip. I had little time left so I rode to the village at a trot, sometimes switching to a gallop. Galloping was easier for me, but not for my poor steed, who became tired all too quickly. Nevertheless, I arrived in the village at dawn. I stopped at the first house and started to put myself and the horse into order. The dirt was frozen solid and it was easy to peel it off my uniform. I also brushed my horse with an improvised hay brush and went in search of HQ.

I reported to the deputy chief of staff of the division and received an order to take twenty riders from the scout squadron and organize the patrolling and defence of 30 kilometres of road, from HQ to the front line. The deputy chief of staff warned me that German ranger units were infiltrating our defences, ambushing and destroying our supply columns.

The riders from the scout squadron were smart and well turned out. Their horses were of the same class as their men: well-fed, strong, and handsome – real riding horses. My poor horse could not compare with them at all. There were two sergeants in my group and we discussed how best to arrange our patrolling routes. We decided to set up base in a village that was right in the middle of the patrolling area. After some formalities our task force left for the village.

I felt quite uncomfortable leading the task force of élite cavalry-men on such a weak horse, especially after one of the sergeants politely pointed out I had put my spurs on inside out. The scouts, however, kept their distance behind me and gave no sign they could see how badly I was riding.

The village we chose as our base was almost intact and there were no troops stationed in it. The men stayed in houses all over the village, while I chose a house in the centre: it was easier to control the two squads from there.

We set the routes for patrolling and made a schedule of patrols. The roads were frozen solid and it was easy for my troopers to travel 15 kilometres one way. A squad would spend one day patrolling and one day resting. I would rarely patrol myself, as I spent most of my time taking care of my horse, which needed much rest and intensive feeding (in order that its ribs might not be so obviously seen through its skin). It was quiet and peaceful on the roads, German ambushes were nowhere to be seen, and I completely relied on the experience and discipline of the sergeants. During this time I had a chance to learn the rules of horse care and cavalry tactics in modern warfare.

Night March

A week quietly passed by. One night I was woken up by an officer. He was the quartermaster of the 24th Guards Cavalry Regiment. It turned out his regiment was relocating and would enter my village for a day's rest. When the regiment arrived, I was summoned to its HQ and duly appointed platoon leader in the AT-gun battery. I was ordered to report to the divisional HQ, send my scouts back to their squadron, and report to the AT-gun battery commander, Guards Senior Lieutenant Agafonov.

I completed all formalities in the divisional HQ and found the battery at the edge of the village. I asked the crews about the commander, and went to the steam bath hut, where the battery commander was staying. I knocked on the door, and a short man with an open Russian face and the manners of a professional officer walked out of the hut. He did not wear a greatcoat and held the rank of senior lieutenant. This was the battery commander. I thought he was about twenty-five years old. An Order of Battle Red Banner was shining on his breast – in those days, this Order was still rare. After listening to my report, he got down to business and suggested I took over the 2nd Platoon. He pointed the platoon out to me and in farewell, told me the regiment would go into battle right after the march, and I should spare the horses in battle – especially the artillery horses, which were the most precious. Yet again, I was reminded that horses were the most important thing in the cavalry: men, guns, and carriages came second place.

I found the platoon and the assistant platoon leader (who was temporarily acting as platoon leader). I informed him of my appointment and ordered him to introduce the personnel and hardware of the platoon to me. There was no time for an official introduction ceremony: the men learned of my appointment from the gun leaders when we were inspecting the guns, horses, and carriages together. The platoon was armed with 45 millimetre anti-tank guns, which were towed by four horses each. Each gun had two ammunition carriages travelling with it. Gun carriages were towed by three horses each. A gun crew consisted of ten men (gun leader, gun-layer, lock operator, loader, ammunition box bearer, four drivers and a groom). There was a total of twenty-three men in the platoon: including platoon leader, assistant platoon leader, and a smith. The platoon was supposed to have thirty-five horses, but some were missing after the previous battles and crews had to travel on the ammunition carriages and gun carriages. We only had eight artillery horses, eight draught horses, and three saddle-horses: a total of nineteen.

Just before our departure we were issued new winter uniforms – light, almost white-coloured sheepskin coats. They looked beautiful and were very warm. However, the weather during that winter was constantly changing from thaw to frost, and very soon our sheepskin coats were wet. As they were made of rawhide sheepskin, they shrank very irregularly as they dried, and soon our men looked like clowns with one sleeve 10 centimetres shorter than the other. Eventually, we had to take off our sheepskin coats and switch back to traditional wool greatcoats with *telogreika* padded jackets underneath. The *telogreika* padded jackets we had were not as thick as the jackets of the 1950s and 1960s, but were rather thin and could be worn under greatcoats.

We spent the whole day taking care of the horses and preparing for the night march. A bugle played the 'saddling' order in the twilight, and the men quickly and silently saddled and harnessed their horses. Gun leaders inspected the horses, carriages, and guns, and reported everything was in readiness for the march. I formed my platoon into a column and led it to the battery, where we took our place in the column behind the first platoon. I again inspected my platoon and reported to the battery commander our readiness for the march. The moon rose in the sky. The soil was frozen solid and the march was not supposed to be difficult. White snow was shining in the moonlight. It squeaked underfoot, making a strange sort of melody when combined with the creaking of the carriage wheels.

Most of my men threw away their gas masks and gas mask bags during the very first hours of the march towards the Front. I was a bit concerned – not because I feared a German gas attack – but because I would have had to pay for the lost gas masks in the event of an inspection! My fellow officers gave me some good advice: 'As soon as we go into battle, write off as much as you can as "destruction by enemy fire."' So I did. After the very first battle, I wrote a report that the carriage carrying all our gas masks was completely destroyed by a direct hit from a German bomb.

I had a very vague idea of what lay in front of me, and a questionable grasp of the tactical role of cavalry – never mind the part my AT-guns were to play in the battle. I only knew one thing: I had to ride at the same speed as the sabre squadrons, supporting them with my fire, and repelling the assaults of the enemy's tanks if they came. But I did not want to think about battles at that moment. I felt good and comfortable. It was nice to breath fresh air, without smoke or the smell of explosions.

The regiment was marching in complete silence. I was with my platoon as a full member of the glorious Guards Cavalry Corps. There was a whole night of marching to the Front. After five or six hours of marching we saw the light of fires on the horizon, set against the black winter sky: fires from villages set ablaze by Germans. We could also see the short flashes of illumination flares as they shot into the sky, and tracer bullets fired from machine-guns. Artillery fire could also be heard in distance: the Front was near.

Our column stopped. Somewhere at its head the bugle call, 'Commanders' Gathering', sounded. Our battery commander spurred his horse and rode off to the regimental HQ. He came back in five minutes, briefed us, and passed on the order: our AT-battery was to be distributed among the squadrons. My platoon was attached to the 3rd and the 4th Squadrons. Without losing any time, I took the third gun of my platoon to the 3rd Squadron, while my deputy platoon leader led the fourth gun to the 4th Squadron. Our regiment was to take up defensive positions along the railway line. This was to be our jump-off point for the coming offensive. We took over the positions of the 3rd Shock Army's infantry, which marched to the rear.

The 3rd Squadron started to dig in on the western slope of a hill adjacent to the railway. We had just enough time to dig in and camouflage our gun before dawn. Together with the gun leader, Guards Sergeant Palanevich, we found a suitable firing position for the 3rd gun. The place was on top of the hill, with no protection from the cold December wind. All the other places did not have a sufficient field of fire.

The crew started to dig into soil that was frozen solid. Their entrenching tools were old and blunt, dating from the Stalingrad battle or before. We were digging trenches for the gun and a shelter for the crew. Our firing position in an open spot, on top of a hill that could be seen for miles from the enemy's side, had only one advantage: a good field of fire on the enemy's first trench and the railway. The departing infantry told us the Germans had an armoured train patrolling the area. Our divisional chief of artillery ordered all batteries to fire at the armoured train when it came and knock it out.

The crew was digging the firing position till dawn. We evened the bottom of the gun's trench, and carefully camouflaged the spoil with snow. Having completed the work, the crew rolled the gun into position, picked up their canteens and went to the field kitchen, leaving only the gun-layer at the position. The kitchen was nearby, in a ravine. The crew received hot buckwheat porridge and frozen bread, which was falling into pieces in the bitter temperature. Men were eating together, just as they were working together. Two or three men were eating from the same canteen. They were taking turns in scooping porridge with their spoons. Having completed their meal, they washed the canteens with snow and drank some hot tea from the same vessels. Afterwards, they started to smoke, hiding the cigarettes in the sleeves of their greatcoats, quietly talking about pre-war life.

The crew had been together for a long time and had grown close during many marches and battles. They knew that a mistake by one man in the crew could cost the lives of them all, and this is what knitted them together. In battle, they acted as one. They knew exactly what to do: they understood each other without words and always obeyed every order of the gun leader.

No one wanted to talk about the coming day. No one wanted to discuss how the enemy would behave, here, in this sector of the

Front, which was completely new and strange to us. Meantime, Winter kept reminding us it was December: the temperature fell constantly through the night; the wind blew, stinging snow into our faces; and the energy and warmth we had received from our hot meal was shivered away, as we grew more and more cold.

The Fritzes fired occasional MG and SMG bursts at our defences. The tracer bullets flew over our heads and into the forest behind, where the supply units of the squadron – horses, carriages, ammunition – were stationed. Sometimes a bullet would hit a stone and ricochet into the dark sky.

A Piece of Paradise

Some 250 metres behind our defences a house was standing. It had
survived the fighting in the area by a sheer miracle. It was a regular
peasant house with a Russian stove. I could see the roof and
windows were intact. I could also see a weak light from a home-
made lamp in one of the windows. This was the house where men
went after receiving permission from their superiors, as if it were
some kind of luxurious resort. They went there for warmth.

The house was packed with men and officers: infantrymen,
cavalrymen, and artillerymen all flocked there. Some men were
sitting, some were sleeping under the table and benches, some
were lying on the stove, some were dozing off on their feet, leaning
against the neighbouring man. The air was so thick that if someone
opened the door, he was almost knocked down by the warm smell
of sweat, old foot rags, and bodies that had not been washed for a
long time. Despite all this, it was a small piece of paradise for men
at the Front. From time to time the door would open and another
frozen man stepped in. But an infantry lieutenant, sitting at the
table, warned everyone to get out of the hut before dawn, because
during the day the place was not safe at all. He warned of strikes
from German artillery and the armoured train, which was patrolling
the area. After he had cautioned everyone, the lieutenant stood up,
ordered all his infantrymen out, and left the house. There was much
more room after they had gone.

But then the door opened and yet another frozen soldier stepped
in. He was of medium height, dressed in a white overall. He carried
a German SMG. Having taken off his mittens and winter hat, he

asked for assistance: 'Brothers, help me! I am almost frozen to death!' 'Where have you come from, so frozen?' I asked him. 'From there!' He pointed at the front line. 'We were ordered to capture a prisoner from the German trenches. We failed. We have permission to warm ourselves up a bit, after that we must go back and lay in ambush until we get a prisoner or freeze to death.' After saying all this, the scout started to climb the stove, without even taking off the overall or leaving his SMG on the floor. I told him not to stay in the house after dawn. He answered something and immediately fell fast asleep. As I was leaving this comfortable house, I ordered my men, who were staying behind, to wake up the scout.

Back at the firing position the blizzard was blowing even stronger. But I had a much more positive view of the world: now I had a little warmth under my greatcoat and in my long boots. The gun leader was checking the gun and ammunition before the battle. The last men of the crew came back from the house. I asked them about the scout. They told me they had woken him up, that he had got up, but then climbed the stove again, saying: 'Whatever happens, let it be! I will sleep for half an hour more!'

At dawn we heard the noise of the approaching German train. The railway was in a ravine on our flank so we could not see what was happening there. Eventually, the armoured train slowly moved out from the ravine and immediately a hail of fire from automatic flak guns and other weapons fell on our hill. I only had to shout: 'Gun and crew, take cover!' And both our gun and the crew were immediately in the trenches. Apparently, the hurricane of fire from the armoured train only lasted for a short time, but to us it seemed there was no end to this firestorm. Did we return fire? Not from this exposed firing position! And despite the fact there were 76 millimetre ZIS-3 guns behind us, they too remained silent. No wonder: the fire from the armoured train was so strong, concentrated, and unexpected, it would have been suicidal to engage the enemy from an open firing position at a distance of less than 1,000 metres.

The armoured train suddenly ceased fire and disappeared back into the ravine. We emerged from our shelter and started to inspect the position. The crew and the gun were intact. The area around our position, however, had been ploughed up by shells. The breastwork was also destroyed. The gunsight's nest was slightly damaged by a splinter, and had the gun-layer not removed the sight at the last second, it would have been destroyed, leaving our gun blind. A similar situation existed in the trenches of the 3rd Squadron. MG nests were hit the hardest. We slowly began to understand the engagement that had just taken place: the enemy train was firing at targets spotted by an artillery observer. We soon located him. He was in a tall tower, some 700 metres behind the railway line. The divisional chief of artillery ordered us to destroy it.

It only took us several seconds to prepare the gun for firing. I ordered: 'At the tower, fragmentation grenade, aim . . . Aim at the centre of the upper part! Fire!' We missed. 'Aim lower! Fire!' Now we hit it. 'Four high explosive grenades, rapid fire!' After the fourth grenade the tower came down. After that I ordered: 'Cease fire, record the destruction of target No. 2, the observer's tower!' We were happy with the results of our fire and more ammunition was brought by carriers from the ravine behind us.

It was only then we noticed our 'piece of paradise' was gone. Instead, there was a heap of bricks and logs in its place. Smoke was curling out from under the ruins. Did that scout manage to get out in time or is he lying there buried beneath the debris? Two infantrymen in boots and leg wrappings sidled up to the ruins, walked around a bit, shook their heads, and left.

We prepared for another visit from the armoured train. I went to the squadron commander's CP and planned the upcoming action and our mutual support. The squadron commander promised me another horse to replace one lost from the gun carriage: it had been killed during the artillery strike. But the armoured train did not reappear. It turned out that scouts and engineers had simply blown up the railway.

As darkness fell, we received an order to relocate to another sector of the Front. We, artillery crews, were ordered to deliver a good strike on the front line German trenches, in order to cover the change of units on our side. Once again, we would be relieving the infantry, and we were happy to oblige, in order to rid ourselves of a certain number of grenades, which were too many and too heavy for our ammunition carriages.

Changing the direction of fire and elevation, we routinely fired at the German positions. We fired four grenades at each elevation and direction, and then switched to another sector. Having fired at least sixty grenades in fifteen minutes, I ordered 'Cease fire!' In complete darkness, our gun took its place in the marching column of the regiment. When passing by the ruined hut, I could not help checking for the scout. Alas, all my hopes were in vain. I could see some pieces of his white overall under the debris. 'What a pity,' I thought, spurring my horse, 'he just wanted a few minutes' peace but got eternal rest instead!'

I rode on, lost in thoughts of heaven or paradise – rewards for a good and blameless life. An old regimental joke came to mind . . .

An elderly maid lived in a village. She had remained a virgin her entire life, as her ambition was to go straight to heaven at the hour of death. The whole village knew how irreproachable she was, and not a single man managed to seduce her.

So her time to die came. She prayed and called for the village priest: 'Father, give me a certificate confirming I remained a virgin my whole life – the whole village knows it and you also know it.' 'What do you need this certificate for?' 'For heaven, father. I want to go to heaven directly, without any bureaucracy.' The priest was confused. It was strange, he had never written such a certificate. But then he decided: 'Times change. You need a certificate for everything these days, even for heaven.' So he wrote her a certificate.

The old maid went home and died peacefully with the certificate in her hand. She went directly to the gates of heaven and found a long queue there. An entire regiment of infantry, killed in battles in Manchuria, was going through the gates of heaven with their rifles and guns. The old woman tried to bypass the queue, but Saint Paul, who was on duty at the gate, shouted: 'Where are you going, old woman, can't you see this whole regiment going in? They deserve to go first, as they were killed on the battlefield.' The old lady stood at the gate and wept. A gun carriage passed by and a happy driver asked her: 'Why are you weeping, old woman?' 'How can't I weep? I was a virgin my whole life, did not have any sex with any man, I even have a certificate, and I cannot get into heaven!' 'Don't worry, old woman, I can help you. Climb on our gun carriage, you will pass for our regimental whore . . .'

Encircled by the Enemy

Our task now was not to sit on the defensive, but to enter gaps in the enemy's defences and push onwards, building on the success of the offensive. This is exactly what we did in the Nevel offensive. Bypassing Lake Ezerische, we breached a crack in the German lines, making our way through awful mud. The corridor was under German artillery, mortar, and even MG fire from both flanks. We moved through this dangerous spot during the night, in complete silence. Speaking and smoking were strictly forbidden. German grenades and bullets whizzed by without harming us, for we were unseen. If it hadn't been for the accursed mud, entering the gap would have been quite tolerable. We were short of horses due to losses in previous battles: the 3rd gun was towed by three horses instead of four; and some members of the crew had to walk, having also lost their horses to enemy fire. When the regiment galloped, they had to jump onto the gun that was towed by the horses.

Meanwhile, the frost was getting stronger, the horses were covered with ice, and men were shivering from the perishing-cold wind. We passed safely through the danger zone and continued our march under the cover of bad weather – stinging snow crystals falling from the sky. By evening, the regiment had concentrated in a long and rather deep ravine. The slope facing the enemy was almost vertical, and this guaranteed our safety from MG and artillery fire. The only thing that could hit us hard was highly accurate mortar fire, but Fritz contented himself with harassing artillery fire, without knowing our precise location.

During another artillery strike the horse under our divisional commander, General N. S. Chepurkin, was killed, while the general himself was wounded. We respected and loved our divisional commander for his caring, almost fatherly, attitude towards simple men and officers. We were all deeply saddened by the wounding of our general, but this did not cause any panic or confusion in the division. Our regiment was preparing for new battles and a new offensive. The field kitchens stood right under the vertical slope of the ravine and started preparing food. Drivers and riders were feeding horses, veterinary officers and blacksmiths were inspecting them. Gun leaders were inspecting the artillery pieces and ammunition carriages. Every man was using the break in operations to do his job. The runners called for commanders to come to the regiment's HQ. Everyone wanted to dry his clothes before the offensive and get a bit warmer: but starting camp fires was strictly forbidden. All the soldiers could do was take off their long boots and rewrap their foot rags.

Our battery commander came back and briefed us in a slow, calm manner. The service and supply units of the regiment were to stay in the ravine, while we were to start the offensive in the evening. The first AT-platoon was to support the 1st and 2nd Squadrons, while the 2nd Platoon was to support the 3rd and the 4th Squadrons. During the offensive there was a possibility of engaging the enemy's armour.

As darkness fell, the regiment quietly formed battle column. The offensive started. I, with my platoon, was in the second echelon of the regiment, the point of which had already made contact with the enemy. But the battle was unsuccessful for us and we had to set up defences. The usual plan of a dashing cavalry raid into the enemy's rear failed this time. The gap made in the German defences by our infantry was shallow – between 10 and 15 kilometres – and our leaders had not bargained for yet another line of enemy trenches. We only realized this when our regiment's scout party ended up under heavy fire from the second German line.

Our defences were located in a low and swampy terrain, and behind our trenches was a small forest. But even the keen frosts did not make ground waters freeze and it was almost impossible to dig in. As soon as we dug some 15 centimetres into the ground there would be water in the hole. So we had to lie in wet, shallow trenches under German shellfire. Yet during the night the water would freeze a little and our greatcoats stuck to the bottom and sides of the trenches. *Valenki*, the felt boots we had just received, were also wet and our foot wrappings froze to them. We all shivered with cold, and in order to warm up at least a little bit, we had to crawl back into the forest. There we could jump and run in order to get warm. Our horses and ammunition carriages were also stationed in the forest. There was a small hill there, and the drivers made some decent trenches on this higher ground, covering the bottoms with the branches of fir trees growing nearby. But the enemy soon located our position, brought in artillery, and started shelling us. German six-barrelled rocket-launchers, *Vanyushas*, were responsible for causing the worst damage to us.

We were in a bad mood. Water in the trenches and a lack of motion had had a bad effect on the health of the men. To make matters worse, Fritz cut the small corridor that was still open in the rear, thus completely encircling us. Supplies of food and ammunition stopped. Men were starving. On the rare occasions the cruel weather allowed our aircraft to fly, 'corn planes' would appear in the sky and drop bags containing hard tack. But they often missed our location and the bags dropped on the German positions. All we could do was dream about the dry tack in German hands. With our dried lips we cursed the damn Fritzes, the weather, the dampness, and the wet, swampy soil that deprived us of any shelter from the enemy's MG and artillery fire. The ubiquitous companions of cold, hunger and filth – lice – came around.

The 4th Squadron commander got drunk and decided to improve our situation by a dashing assault on the German positions without even asking permission from the regimental commander. He ordered his squadron to attack the Germans, and walked openly in front of the assault line. He led his squadron towards the German positions without any preliminary artillery strike or even a proper machine-gun support. Some 20 metres from the German trenches the squadron commander was killed and the assault stopped due to concentrated German automatic fire. The survivors from the 4th Squadron crawled back to their trenches.

The regimental commander was furious about the incident, but there was no one to be tried: the guilty officer was lying dead on the battlefield. We decided to evacuate the dead from the battlefield during the night, in order to avoid more losses. Our morale was getting low – hunger and cold did their job.

When inspecting the camp of my drivers and ammunition carriages in the forest, I noticed a small pillar of smoke from a camp-fire. The smoke was coming out of a shallow ravine. When I came a bit closer I saw a group of officers making themselves warm at a small campfire, which was dubbed 'Tashkent'. Among the officers there was a medic from our regiment. Some officers were sitting at the fire naked from the waist up, frying their tunics and undershirts, while lice – which were swarming all over the garments – exploded with loud snaps to the great amusement of all. The officers were shivering and cursing the war with the worst obscenities.

I also sat at the fire, warming my frozen hands. The medic, a captain, proposed another way of fighting lice without taking tunics off. He pulled a bandage out of his pocket, unfolded it, and put the lower end of it through the collar of his tunic. After sitting like that for some ten to fifteen minutes, he pulled the bandage out. There were about a dozen lice sitting on the bandage. The captain cut off this part of bandage with scissors and threw it into the fire. The bandage burnt together with the lice.

All the officers liked this new way of 'fishing' for lice on a piece of bandage and they started doing it themselves. But of course, it was in vain, as the lice multiplied on a dirty and weakened body much faster than we could catch them with a 'lice rod'. We all needed a good wash and disinfestation, but it was impossible in our situation – even the smoke from a small campfire like 'Tashkent' would draw artillery fire of the enemy.

It was time for me to leave the campfire and return to the gun. The situation was difficult for us, as the Germans could launch an assault on our positions at any moment: and so I had no choice but to hurry back to the gun.

The gun leader, Guards Sergeant Palanevitch, was setting up a good camp for the night, ordering the crew to bring dry firewood and fir tree branches to the small dugouts at the gun. The evening was misty – fog was hanging low – and we could not see the enemy's positions clearly.

I had fixed my small trench some 10 metres from the gun, next to a small hillock. I exchanged the wet fir tree branches for dry ones. A driver brought me my dinner, which was also my lunch. The thin millet soup in the canteen was still hot. I put the canteen on the hillock and ate it with great relish, despite the fact it had no taste, and neither had the accompanying bread, which was frozen solid. But the food made me warm and I decided to make my skirmisher's trench wider before the next German artillery strike.

When I removed the top layer of snow from the hillock, in order to dig, I came across a piece of German greatcoat. When I burrowed deeper into the snow, I realized the small hillock next to my trench was, in fact, the frozen body of a dead German soldier. I was very unhappy to have such a neighbour! Especially unpleasant was the fact I had just used this body as a table for my dinner. Also, during the previous night I had used the dead body as protection from the wind, pressing my back against it. Well, I would have to dig myself a new trench and camouflage the old one with snow. But for now, I sank into my cold, wet, skirmishers trench. Somehow I managed to fall asleep.

I woke up some time around midnight, frozen to my bones and shivering. At that moment I decided, 'Whatever, I don't care about security anymore,' and went into the forest to lay down in our ammunition carriage under a layer of hay.

I was woken up by the thunder of German bombs, which were exploding all around: yet another bombardment from Fritz's six-barrelled *Vanyusha* rocket-launcher. The horses that were still harnessed to the carriage were galloping through the forest like crazy. I jumped up and still half-asleep, managed to stop the horses. One of them was badly wounded; another two had deep gashes on their flanks with blood oozing from them. The sides of the ammunition carriage were shattered with splinters. I called for the drivers to unharness the crippled horse, which had dropped to the ground. A sergeant who came running from the gun's firing position said the driver was asleep in a trench underneath where the carriage stood. I did not believe him. It just could not be that a disciplined, business-like old soldier like my driver would sleep after such a hellish strike of *Vanyusha*. While the sergeant was unharnessing the horse, I ran to the trench. The driver was lying there motionless. At first, I, too, thought he was asleep: but when I shook him, in order to rouse him, I realized he was dead. The sergeant walked up, unbuttoned the driver's greatcoat and tunic, and we saw a large splinter hole in his chest, right where his heart was. We picked up his ID and other documents and buried him in the trench, putting a small stick with a wooden sign on the grave.

I am still amazed how it could happen that I – being in the ammunition carriage, about half a metre from the ground – survived and was not even wounded (although my greatcoat was torn in several places by splinters), while the driver, who was in a trench under the carriage, was killed.

Before we could complete the funeral of the driver, we heard the awful screeching sound of *Vanyusha* again, and yet another series of deadly projectiles fell on the forest not far from us. The six-barrelled rocket-launcher was so dangerous in the forest because its projectiles exploded above ground as they slammed into the trees, sending splinters flying downwards, which could kill men hiding in trenches.

The crippled horse had to be butchered and that night all units got fresh horse meat for dinner.

We only spent a few days in our tiny pocket, encircled by the enemy, but they probably held the worst memories of the whole war for most us (though not for me, as I had lived through the siege of Leningrad). But one evening in November 1943, we received the order to withdraw from our positions and break out. As it happened, the encirclement was broken at the first attempt by our advance guard and during the night the entire regiment left its positions and quietly slipped through the gap. Now we were all in high spirits, as we knew we could finally wash ourselves and receive decent food.

But when leaving our positions, I made a big mistake that could have cost me life, or even worse, my liberty. After I had placed Palanevitch's gun and ammunition carriages in the regiment's column, I decided to check whether another gun of my platoon, under Guards Sergeant Petrenko, had been informed of our departure: for, had the gun with its crew remained in the pocket, I would have been held responsible. At that time I had no weapon – not even a pistol – so I took a carbine from my soldier and went back to the former positions of the 4th Squadron. It was completely quiet – just the wind whistling in the tops of the trees and snow creaking under my feet. I put the cartridge into the chamber and carefully approached the positions of my gun. There was not a single living soul in the trenches. The tracks in the snow clearly indicated that the gun crew had left together with the squadron. The enemy was also quiet: they did not know about our retreat, otherwise they would have attacked and made us fight – something we did not need at that moment.

As usual, the Germans were firing flares and harassing us with MG and artillery fire. However, I could easily run into a German patrol and, of course, I would not have been able to resist them for long with one puny carbine. So I slung the weapon behind my back and ran off to find the regiment. Suddenly, all was quiet, and I realized that if it began to snow, the road would soon disappear and I would never find my way in the darkness. My heart began beating like crazy. I felt the blood pumping at my temples. In order to catch my breath, I began walking – all the time thinking that I could be left behind. This thought propelled me forward till I broke into a run and – to my great relief – I bumped into the rearguard of the regiment. It was like reaching my father's door.

After giving it some thought, I decided not to report the episode concerning my search for the gun. I was scared of a scolding from my superiors. But my report on the condition of my platoon was turned in with some delay. Luckily, however, my absence had gone unnoticed.

Driver Vedernikov

As we made it out of the encirclement, we continued a slow march
towards our concentration area. Even before we reached our destination, during a break, the medics set up a field bath and
insect-cleansing operation. Where and how the medics got the steel
barrels for the 'bug killers', and how on earth they managed to set
everything up in a matter hours in the field – this remains yet another
mystery of the Red Army in the past war. Such an operation required
management and leadership skills similar to those needed in battle.
Deputy platoon leaders, squad leaders, sergeant majors, all followed
the instructions of the medics. After bathing, we were given clean
underwear. Such field bath days were like holidays to us, and they
boosted our morale better than any regimental orchestra playing
marches.

During the next day's break, it was the veterinary officers' turn.
Together with the blacksmiths they inspected all the horses in our
unit. Every platoon had its own blacksmith, who was a crucial
person in our battle-readiness. A horse with bad shoes is a liability
in battle. Meanwhile, gun leaders used every free minute for the
inspection of artillery pieces, ammunition carriages, small arms, and
harnesses. No one knew how long a break from battle might be:
only if we were stationed in some village, far away from the Front,
could one hope a break would last for a week.

But our regiment stopped for a prolonged break at a village in the
Vitebsk area. The village was reasonably well preserved after
German occupation. Our battery lodged in a separate building
about half a kilometre from the village and the regimental HQ.

Officers and supply units (that is to say, our kitchen, food carriages, veterinary, and medical units) stayed in the house, while the crews built some light shelters for themselves in the field. The horses remained outdoors.

The local population lived very poorly after the German occupation. They no longer had cattle, straw, hay, or anything else. Only potatoes, garlic, plus a little rye bread: but for these, they would have starved. As the villagers could not provide us with food, both we and our horses had a hungry time. The food we received for the horses – 8 kilograms of barley for artillery horses, 6 for draught horses, and 4 for riders' horses – could not compensate for the absence of raw nutrition in the form of hay or straw. And so the horses started to lose weight. In the course of a single day they would chew up the stout logs they were tied to. We were facing a massive problem. The regiment's HQ proposed clearing the fields of snow and gathering grass from the previous year. The very first attempt to do so came to nothing: the grass was frozen solid to the ground.

Our battery commander, Senior Lieutenant Agafonov, gathered the platoon leaders, sergeant major, and veterinary officers for a council. He proposed taking straw from the roofs of destroyed or abandoned huts. It was a good idea and everyone supported it. Meanwhile, I was sent into another district, some 30 kilometres from our village, in order to look for hay. I was given four carriages and the most experienced drivers. We took all the necessary equipment – axes, saws, ropes – plus enough hard tack for two days, and set off north. We headed north because we thought there were more destroyed villages in that direction. The morning was cold and the wheels of the carriages squeaked like a strange orchestra.

I was on the first carriage and the last was led by Vedernikov: a strong, quiet, and slow person, who was also a very good and business-like driver. The morning was beautiful, with shining sun and sparkling snow. After we journeyed some 20 kilometres from our village, we entered an area where battles had just ended. There was plenty of wrecked military hardware lying under the snow. About 100 metres from the road there lay a dead horse. It looked rather fat and well-fed, lying with its feet in the air. Vedernikov's carriage stopped, while Vedernikov himself grabbed an axe and ran off from the road, sinking in deep snow. The road made a turn at this spot, and I shouted to Vedernikov that he should not take a long time there. But he caught up with us in half an hour and we continued our journey. I was almost falling asleep on the first carriage and had assumed that Vedernikov had simply wanted to answer the call of nature: but why, then, did he take an axe with him?

The weather changed for the worse in the evening: a howling wind brought heavy snow and the road was covered with drifts. As darkness fell, we lost the road entirely, and moved through an open field, hoping for luck. Suddenly, we ran into a destroyed barn. It did not have any walls and its roof was lying on the ground. As luck would have it, it was made of straw. I jumped off the carriage and inspected the straw. It was old, of course, but it was quite acceptable for the horses. I threw some under the feet of our horses and they devoured it instantly. We did not have to look any further. Despite the blizzard, it only took us a few minutes to take the straw off the roof and load it onto the carriages. We filled two carriages, and I was very pleased, as this was almost half the quota given to me by the battery commander. I ordered the drivers of the laden carriages to drive back to the regiment immediately. Meanwhile, the rest of us fed the remaining straw to our horses, found the road, and continued to search for our luck.

The wind grew even stronger. We had to find shelter. Having wandered in darkness for about an hour, we heard the sound of dogs barking in the distance. We drove in that direction and soon arrived at a solitary house. As it turned out, this was the last remaining building of what used to be a whole village. There was a light in the window. We tied the horses to the fence and knocked at the door. It was opened by a woman. She looked old but her voice sounded young, as she invited us to come in. Inside it was warm. A dim light shone from an old kerosene lamp on the table. Its meagre light illuminated the table only: the rest of the room was in darkness. We were frozen to our bones and happy to be out of the raging blizzard.

The landlady welcomed us and told us we could rest in her house and get warmer. Without any ceremony she told me I could sleep on the bed together with her children, while the soldiers were going about their business. I did not wait for a second invitation and immediately lay down on a bed next to several children who were sleeping in a pile. Within moments, I, too, was fast asleep.

I was awoken by Vedernikov, who invited me for a meal. There was a tasty smell of boiled meat and potatoes with garlic coming from the table. Vedernikov invited everyone in the house to eat with us. There were so many of them they could not squeeze round the large table. I quickly washed my hands and sat down to eat.

Vedernikov was the master of ceremony at the table. He gave everyone a large piece of boiled meat. The boiled potatoes were in two large pots at the corner of the table and everyone could take as much as they wanted. The children were especially happy – they woke up as soon as they sensed the smell of meat. They jumped up from the bed, wearing only their shirts, and sat on their mothers' laps. 'Where on earth did he get all this meat?' I silently asked myself. This question was repeated aloud by a young woman, whom Vedernikov was inviting to eat. Vedernikov did not think long and answered that she should not worry as we soldiers were very well supplied with food and were always ready to share food with people in need. Another woman suspected something and asked: 'Is it horse meat? I could never eat horse meat, I would throw up immediately!'

However, no one really paid attention to these questions and doubts: everyone ate the meat and no one threw up. On the contrary, everyone had a great appetite, eating large pieces of meat together with potatoes and garlic. The children were eating with even greater relish than we. Sometimes they looked at us timidly with their big eyes. The meat was soft and juicy. The woman, who suspected the meat to be horseflesh, was especially happy.

As we talked during our meal, it turned out that in addition to the owner, there were three more families staying in the house. Their own homes were destroyed. There were only women and small children. All the men of the village were either in the Army or in partisan units. They had taken all the cattle with them. The house had remained intact only by a miracle: even the dog had survived – its barking had led us to the house in darkness.

Only after I had eaten the dinner cooked by Vedernikov, did I realize where he had got the meat from. I recalled the dead horse on the road, how Vedernikov had jumped off the carriage with an axe, and everything became clear. Luckily, there was a severe frost, and the horse meat was frozen solid, just like in a refrigerator. Everyone thanked Vedernikov for such a great dinner, saying they had not had such a meal since the outbreak of the war.

It grew light outdoors, the blizzard was over and we had to

continue our journey. We thanked the owner of the house and left them a can of Spam. After that we continued our hunt for straw. After long searches in the fields we spotted an old haystack at the edge of a forest. We loaded it onto the carriages and arrived at our unit before dusk. Our commander, Guards Senior Lieutenant Agafonov, was delighted and did not even argue or object when the regiment's chief of staff arrived and ordered him to give one carriage of straw to the regimental HQ.

Miracle of Nature

In the evening of 27 January 1944, our battery's clerk found me and told me I had to report to the regimental HQ immediately. He did not know why they wanted to see me. The driver brought me a saddled horse and we galloped off. The duty officer was already waiting for me when I arrived, and immediately sent me to the political officer of the regiment, Guards Major Vydajko.

The major was popular with everyone: he was a very open, simple, and caring person. He told me to sit down and explained why I had been summoned. Apparently, the entire 5th Guards Cavalry Division was to gather for a meeting the following day. The meeting was dedicated to the complete destruction of the German siege around Leningrad: it seemed I was the only person from the city in the entire division!

Next day, 28 January, all the regiments of the division stood in parade formation on a large field. Right after the speech by the political officer of the division, the floor was given to me. I spoke about the siege. I told of the heroic people of Leningrad, who were dying from cold, hunger, German bombs and shells, but who refused to surrender. I told of how the citizens had built defences, how they threw incendiary bombs from the roofs of their homes, how they worked round the clock at factories and plants. At the end of my speech I encouraged all the Guardsmen to avenge those who had died in the siege of Leningrad. The meeting was concluded with a loud 'Hurrah!' to the glorious Red Army and our Party. The division's orchestra played the national anthem of the

Soviet Union. The regiments marched to their camps with flying banners, escorted by the strains of military marches.

It was around this time the regiment started to receive replacements of both men and horses. The young men were mostly from the Poltava area in the Ukraine and the Saratov area in southern Russia. Our cavalry corps had been ordered to relocate, so the new recruits had to learn the ropes and get used to field life on the march.

The replacement horses we received were a gift to the Soviet Union from Mongolia. These mounts were quite small and not very domesticated. They did not want to eat barley from bags and refused to drink water from the tarpaulin buckets we hung round their necks. Yet this was a crucial element of cavalry practice: we had to feed our horses this way. Consequently, the Mongolian ponies started to sicken and die. Our regimental commander, Guards Lieutenant Colonel Tkalenko, gathered the squadron commanders. He wanted to shame them over their apparent lack of care, and announced that some of the 'Mongolians' were to be given to the artillery batteries, so that gunners could teach cavalrymen how to treat horses. After this we received around forty Mongolian horses, both for the gun carriages and the crews. But none of our veterans wanted a Mongolian horse – this miracle of nature – and they were all given away to the recruits. That was the start of our nightmare: for we had to train up the new soldiers, while they, in turn, had to train the 'Mongolians'. After many difficulties and some losses (about five or six horses died) we managed to teach the Mongolian horses to eat barley from the bags, drink water from the buckets, and keep formation. But I should really praise the Mongolian ponies: though they were too short for the taste of dandy cavalry officers, they were very enduring on the march and fast in battles.

Give Me a Rifle With a Twisted Barrel

We normally marched at night. During the day, we rested in forests or ravines, next to some settlement. Night marching was a tough ordeal for our new soldiers, as they had to stay awake but also feed and groom the horses during the day, as well as clean their weapons. Drivers of the gun and ammunition carriages had even more tasks to do: each one of them had two or three horses to care for. Those on duty had even more chores.

If we had to leave the forest during daylight, we had to change our cavalry shoulder boards for some other type: like infantry, with raspberry piping, or artillery, with red piping. Such secrecy was necessary in order to conceal the direction of the main thrust of our forces, so the enemy could not prepare his defences. It was especially important that the presence of cavalrymen be hidden, for we had a specific task: our role was not to remain in defence, but to enter gaps in the German line created by our infantry. We had to ride as far possible into the enemy's rear, exploiting the success of the offensive. Thus, if a large cavalry unit arrived at a certain sector of the Front, one could expect an attack to be imminent.

At one of our daily breaks we received an order to return all captured small arms: only gun leaders were permitted to keep sub-machine guns. It was always like that. As soon as we entered a gap in the German defences and went into battle, we would pile our cavalry carbines on a carriage and pick up sub-machine guns – be they Russian or German. After the fighting, we always received an order to hand in all weapons that did not fit our field manuals and

switched back to carbines. Gun-layers were also supposed to get
pistols, but they never got them during the whole war.

In place of the weapons that we handed in, the crews and drivers
received the Model 1891 Mosin-Nagant infantry long-barrelled
rifles, which did not suit anyone in the cavalry. But orders are not
to be discussed and we began cleaning the weapons. The rifles
were old and in poor shape. One of the young soldiers was
cleaning his barrel with a ramrod and slammed it in with such
force that he could not get it out. He was almost weeping with
frustration. I had to help him out. I ordered him to take a bullet
out of the cartridge. I put this improvised blank cartridge into the
chamber, closed the lock, and walked away from my men. Then I
fired the ramrod into the air. This, of course, was against all regulations: but I had no other choice. We were doing all this in a spot
between a forest and a road. After cleaning the rifles, we had to
adjust their sights by test-firing them. We test-fired the rifles at
targets set below the brow of a hill, between the forest and the
road. As we were test-firing the rifles, a strange lieutenant colonel
(it turned out this was the division's NKVD officer) rode up to us
and gave us a scolding. He claimed that as he was riding along the
road our bullets had been whistling around him. We looked at
each other. I pointed out the direction of our fire to the lieutenant
colonel, but he did not believe me, shook his fist at us, and rode
off. One could not argue with the division's NKVD officer so I
kept my mouth shut.

As I was inspecting the inner parts of another 'new' rifle, I saw
the barrel was not straight. This was why the bullets fired from
this weapon had veered towards the road. My deputy platoon
leader was not very sorry about this and added that he knew who
should get this rifle: for there was one young soldier among the
new replacements who would be happy to fire at the enemy from
behind a corner. It was just like in a joke we had: 'Yes I want to
fight the war! I want to be in a supply unit on the very last
carriage from the Front! Also, give me a rifle with a twisted barrel
so I can fire at the enemy from behind a corner!' After that
everyone started telling jokes and funny stories. The gun leader
told the following anecdote: 'I personally saw the following situation. Our neighbouring unit was infantry. The company
commander rallied his men for the assault, shouting, "Forward,

my eagles of Russia!" Everyone stood up, except for two Jewish soldiers. The political officer asked them: "Why are you sitting? The whole company is advancing!" The answer was: "We are lions of Zion – the order was given to eagles of Russia."'

Private Balatski

After an exhausting night march we approached a village in complete darkness. It was cold and a bitter wind was blowing stinging snow crystals straight into our faces. Of course, everyone longed to step into a warm house just for five minutes, but in fact, this was the worst thing men could do given their condition. Consequently, Battery Commander Agafonov passed a strict order along the column, forbidding anyone to dismount and enter the houses. I warned the gun leaders, telling them to keep an eye on the new soldiers. We officers had to look after our men like shepherds: a hard task in complete darkness.

When we entered the village, as ill luck would have it, we stopped for some ten minutes. As usual after a halt, our column moved off at a prolonged trot, which lasted some time. When the regiment slowed down, the officers began checking their personnel. I could find no trace of a young soldier in my platoon named Balatski. He had arrived with the new replacements and had trouble with discipline. I sent his gun leader, Guards Sergeant Petrenko to search for him. Petrenko came back in half an hour, having failed to find the soldier. Losing a man, especially in a non-battle environment, is an emergency and a catastrophe for the whole unit. This is why I left word with the battery commander and rode off to search for Balatski myself. I rode back down the column shouting: 'Balatski! Balatski!' There was no answer. Our divisional column ended and after a short distance I encountered the dense masses of the 6th Guards Cavalry Division. But Balatski was nowhere to be seen.

It was only when I came within a couple of kilometres from that ill-fated village I heard an answer to my shouting: 'I'm here! I'm here!' I felt a huge sense of relief. I directed my horse towards the voice. There, on the side of the road, was the silhouette of a small soldier. It was Balatski, who was missing his horse. I quickly asked him the reason for his absence and ordered him to hold on fast to my stirrups. We quickly caught up with the battery. I was happy I had found him, but at the same time I was furious with him for his actions.

Everything had happened just like Agafonov, our battery commander, had feared. When we stopped in the village, Balatski, who was frozen to his bones, dismounted, and walked up to the nearest house. There he tied his Mongolian horse to the fence and entered the dwelling, in order warm himself. Within moments he had fallen asleep on a chair. When he awoke and ran out of the house, his horse had gone: either it had managed to break free, or it had been taken away by the men of another regiment. Balatski tried to find the horse, but it was impossible to do so in a dark night as black as pitch. Balatski feared he would be accused of desertion and set off on foot to catch up with our regiment.

In the cavalry, caring for a horse is one of the primary responsibilities for any soldier. I don't know if Balatski knew anything about it but he certainly looked very pitiful and lost. He understood his guilt and was ready to run, holding on to my stirrup, in order to catch up with the regiment. He was nearly crying.

In the battles that lay ahead of us Balatski could do without a horse, as he was a gun crew member and could ride on the carriage of the gun. Nevertheless, I punished Balatski severely and ordered him to find a new mount in the very first battle. This he did, finding himself both horse and saddle. He turned out to be a good soldier.

Live Ammunition

On one of those spring days I received an order to prepare one of my guns for a demonstration at a weaponry display for our corps. All the participants of the display were given their own sector of fire, at a target and range of their choosing. Our gun's targets were three dummy MGs at a distance of 1.5 kilometres. Next to us was a 76 millimetre gun from the regimental artillery, which also had its own target: a dummy MG and a dummy bunker. We were all given one day to build the targets and dig in our gun. I measured the distance to the targets with my steps and set the sight very precisely. Gun leader, Guards Sergeant Palanevich, drew a map of reference points and glued it to the inside of our gun's armoured shield.

Early in the morning, the display was ready, and all the weapons of our corps – from light machine-guns to T-34 tanks – were standing at the edge of the firing range, ready for action. The top brass of the corps appeared, moving in one large group from one weapon to another. The small arms completed their firing exercises. The generals walked up to our gun. Among them I noticed our regimental commander and our divisional commander. I briefly and clearly introduced my gun and its technical characteristics, then I requested permission to open fire. Permission was granted and I gave my usual order, first identifying the target: 'Reference point number one, 0 – 30 to the right, sight settings . . .' and so on. Then I ordered: 'at the machine-gun, grenade, fragmentation, one grenade, fire!' After the loud snap of the lock there was a shot, and I saw the dummy machine-gun flying in to the air! It only took four grenades to destroy the three targets. Even without binoculars, one could clearly see the wooden dummies being blasted to pieces by direct hits.

The generals liked my shooting and ordered me to fire at other targets. I reported that those targets were not mine, but the generals ordered me to destroy one of the targets of the regimental artillery. So I did just that: destroying the target with just one grenade.

Several days later we had an all-out combat training on regimental level with live ammunition. It was almost like the real thing: as close to genuine action as we could get. Live ammunition was necessary not only for new soldiers, but also for our new horses. 'Green' horses – which had not yet seen action – were especially dangerous in gun teams: for as they jumped and fretted with the sound of nearby explosions their harnesses became entangled, preventing speedy deployment of the gun in a battle situation.

After the battle training, the crews cleaned their guns and small arms, again preparing for the march. At the end of our break, *Komsomol* (Lenin's Youth organization) meetings took place in all units. At the *Komsomol* meeting of our battery I was elected the *Komsomol* secretary of the battery – or, as they were jokingly called among front line troops, a 'Komsomol god'. And so, in addition to my duties as platoon leader, I now had duties in political life.

During the training, a tragic incident took place. A mortar battery was supporting an assault squadron when a shell suddenly disintegrated in mid-flight, falling on the advancing line. Five men were killed and wounded. Despite these losses, training with live ammunition was necessary, as the lessons men learned during such intensive and realistic simulations saved hundreds of lives in real action. It is always painful for me to recall our battles, when the highest losses were always among the green, untried soldiers.

An unpleasant thing also happened in my own platoon during that exercise with live ammunition. The training was physically and psychologically hard for the men, especially in mounted artillery, as one had to take care of horses, guns, personal weapons, and so on. The soldiers were exhausted. One of the men from my platoon could not take it and deserted. But he did not desert to the rear – he merely walked off towards the front line and joined an infantry unit. He did not tell anyone about his plans, so I had to report his disappearance as a desertion. He was only found after the liberation of Belorussia, and was brought back to our unit unarmed and under arrest. They set up a court martial for him, but he did not say a word:

he just gave the military judges a letter of recommendation from the infantry unit he had joined. The recommendation was excellent – his platoon leader even recommended him for a decoration – but the fact of the desertion could not be ignored and the man was sent to a penal company. And yet, as it happened, the man was happy: for the penal company was attached to his old infantry unit and he knew everyone there.

In a Forest at the Front Line

About two days before we were due to leave, the landlady in the house where we were staying predicted our departure. How on earth did those women always know top secret information before we did? It is still a mystery to me! They could not know it through anyone in the regiment's staff, as they themselves received orders at the very last moment.

But our landlady was right: two days later the 'Saddle!' order came, and within an hour we had formed a column on the road. We marched the whole night, and in the morning we were loaded on a train. We headed south. It was nice and comfortable in the train. Both men and horses had rest. It was great to be on the train, with the rhythmic noise of the wheels – and my whole platoon in one place! During short breaks men jumped out to stretch their legs, pick up some straw, and find water for the horses or food for their bellies. My only trouble was making sure no one got left behind.

In the evening, our train stopped in the middle of an open field and we received an order to disembark. Again we had to march. Soon we reached our temporary home – in an old forest. The trees in that forest were mighty and old; the sunlight could barely penetrate the masses of leaves. There were no branches growing on the lower parts of the trees, and there was no grass on the ground. It was like being in the great hall of some fairy-tale castle! One could not find a better place for the concealment of a large number of troops – it was impossible to spot us from the air. There were many more units – infantry, service, and supply – in that forest. We saw artists from some theatre giving a performance from an improvised stage on the back of a truck. That was the first time I heard a waltz called, 'In a Forest at the Front Line.' As it was actually happening in a forest near the front line, the impression of that piece of music was overwhelming.

A yellow leaf is falling
From a birch tree, light and clean,
A harmonist is playing
An old waltz, 'Autumn Dream'.
The harmonica is sighing and weeping
And if they were asleep,
My friends are sitting and listening –
My dear battle friends.
With this waltz on a spring day
We went to a village dance,
With this waltz in our homeland
We had our first romance.
With this waltz we were looking
Into our beloved's eyes with care,
With this waltz we were grieving
When our girlfriend was not there.
Again this waltz is playing
In a forest at the front line,
And each one is recalling
A dear and precious life.
Each one is thinking of his own,
Recalling his first spring
And each one knows – it can return,
Just if we win this war.
So let the joy of our pre-war life
Light our way here, in war!
And if we are to fall and die –
We can only die but once!
But may death here in smoke and fire
Not scare a man in the fight,
And let each one of us aspire
To do our duty right.
So, friends, if our turn has come –
Let our steel be hard!

Keep our hands clean and strong
And keep our hearts on guard!
Our turn has come, the time is here,
Let's go, my friends, let's go!
For all the dear memories
And peaceful life we hope for!
A yellow leaf is falling
From a birch tree, light and clean,
A harmonist is playing
An old waltz, 'Autumn Dream'.
The harmonica is sighing and weeping
And if they were asleep,
My friends are sitting and listening
My dear battle friends . . .

A Whole Pouch of Tobacco

Yet again we had to march to another place along the front line: this time to the northwest. Our new area of concentration was a young birch forest with many nice sunny clearings covered with green grass. It was beautiful, sunny, summer weather. But we were at war and forbidden to leave the forest. Camouflage requirements were tightened. If anyone did leave the forest – on duty or for some other important reason – they had to remove their spurs and cavalry shoulder boards, replacing them with those of some other branch of the service. The emblem of our corps (at that time it was a horse's head with the divisional number) also had to be removed from trucks and other pieces of equipment that left the forest.

Due to this minimization of traffic in the area, we received fewer supplies. Smokers suffered the worst, as there was no tobacco left. Even at the regimental HQ, officers were smoking the pitiful remains of tobacco scraped up from the bottoms of their pockets and tobacco pouches. It was with some amazement, then, that I noticed my regimental artillery platoon leader, Guards Lieutenant Kuchmar, had a whole pouch of tobacco. He was smiling and slowly stuffing his pipe. He could not live without his pipe and always carried it with him. As I was his best friend, I immediately prepared a piece of paper – half the size of a leaf from a notepad – and put my hand into his tobacco pouch. I rolled the cigarette, which was as thick as a dog's leg. I got a light from his pipe, and at the very first draw of air into my lungs, I almost suffocated from the horrible bitter smell. A shower of tears rained from my eyes. Kuchmar was still smiling and smoking his favourite pipe, looking at me and at other boys who lined up for free tobacco. Those who took free tobacco from a friend were called 'shooters'. I caught my breath and threw the damn cigarette on the ground. After that I received an answer concerning the origin of this nasty mixture.

It turned out that before the war Kuchmar worked as an engineer at a factory in the Urals region and could not live a single day without smoking his pipe. In order to compensate for a lack of tobacco, he made his own smoking blend from old birch leaves and dry sawdust. The mixture he invented looked like something between *makhorka* [literally, 'cheap tobacco' – editor's note] and the light tobaccos of lower sorts. I cannot imagine how he could smoke that stuff! When recalling the incident I still have bitterness in my mouth and stinging in my throat.

Silhouette of a Soldier

Here we were again marching: this time towards front line, our final stop before battle. We were quite close to the Front and the regiment was marching in daylight – a rare event during redeployment. The sun was shining brightly, a cool breeze blew from the fields. To the left of us there was a noisy column of tanks and self-propelled guns from the III Mechanized Corps. Our column slowed down and finally stopped. The 'Dismount' order came from the head of the column, repeated by every man down the long line. Riders quickly jumped off their horses. It was good to stand on solid soil after a long ride.

As we dismounted, we saw a strange mark on the surface of the road. It was the silhouette of a soldier, with legs and arms spread to his sides, head facing west, toward the front line. The soldier had been crushed into the surface of the road so that his remains were no thicker than a sheet of paper. Hundreds of tanks and trucks must have driven over his body, making him one with the road. Judging by the tatters of his uniform, he had been an infantryman. What had happened to this man? Was he a tank rider who got wounded and fell off his tank? Or was he killed? There was no answer. The only answer was to fight even harder, take revenge on the Germans for all the grief and misery they had brought to our longsuffering Motherland. We had to avenge all the fallen of this holy war.

The soldier's company commander had probably reported him 'missing in action' – there would have been little time to check once the offensive was underway, and his job was to press forward without giving the enemy any respite. The soldier's friends probably drank a shot of vodka for his rest in peace and marched forward. And that was it.

Our column began to move. The 'Mount!' order was again passed on by everyone along the column. The regiment broke into a trot and continued its march towards the front line.

Avalanche

The last night before entering the gap in the German defences came. Waiting in the jump-off area was the hardest thing for every soldier. Men and officers wanted to go into action as quickly as possible. Everyone knew that by the end of the operation only one third of the regiment would remain: two-thirds would be killed or wounded. The dead would forever remain on the battlefield and the wounded could be crippled, carrying a mark of this holy war for the rest of their lives. We heard artillery fire in the distance. No one could sleep during this last night.

On the morning of 23 June 1944 our Combined Mechanized Cavalry Group (III Guards Cavalry Corps and III Guards Mechanized Corps) entered the gap that had been made in the German defences by tank and infantry units. The 2nd Squadron of our regiment was the first one to go into battle at Bogushevsk. This squadron, under Guards Senior Sergeant Oleinikov, was in the regiment's point and suddenly ran into Fritz's defensive perimeter around the town. Oleinikov made a bold decision: two sabre platoons dismounted and began a firefight with the Germans, distracting their attention, while Oleinikov and the two remaining sabre platoons bypassed the German defences and stormed them from the rear, on horseback with sabres drawn. The Germans fled in panic.

After Bogushevsk came a large village and an important railway junction called Smolyany. When we approached it, the village was burning, set on fire by Germans. This was the battle in which the 2nd gun of our battery, under Guards Sergeant Malakhov, had to do a lot of work. The 2nd Squadron, which Malakhov was supporting, was supposed to capture the eastern outskirts of the village. The perimeter was defended by some twenty Germans armed with a light machine-gun. Our squadron was pinned down. When Malakhov saw this, he started moving his gun forward, to an open firing position. The Germans spotted his gun and concentrated all their fire on the crew. German artillery joined the attempt to destroy Malakhov's lone 45 millimetre gun, but the Fritzes missed and Malakhov opened fire. He destroyed the German machine-gun and continued to support the squadron with direct fire. He also managed to destroy a German ammunition truck. After the destruction of the machine-gun, the squadron charged forward and easily captured Smolyany. Malakhov received the Order of the Red Star for that battle.

But we were advancing in the second echelon of the regiment and did not see too much action at first. There were rumours circulating in the division we could encounter a cavalry brigade manned by Vlasov's men – those who had betrayed our country and agreed to fight on the German side [Lieutenant General A.A. Vlasov (1901–1946) was the highest-ranking defector from the Red Army during the Great Patriotic War. Following his surrender to the Germans in 1942, he agreed to collaborate with the Wehrmacht, subsequently raising a 'Russian Liberation Army' composed of POWs. Vlasov was eventually captured by the Red Army, tried, and executed by hanging – editor's note]. During training sessions I had seen a sabre charge performed by two or three squadrons simultaneously – it was a fearsome sight. A high-speed charge by massed horsemen was dubbed an 'avalanche' in the Russian cavalry, and I realized that if my two 45 millimetre guns came under attack by Vlasov's troopers, we would have had no chance of survival: they would be too fast for our fragmentation shells to stop them. So I requested grapeshot from the ammunition depot. But such shells were not available from the regimental depot and I was left feeling quite uneasy. One day, during our march in the second echelon, I spotted an abandoned Soviet-made 45 millimetre gun at the side of the road. It looked like the Germans had captured it and used it for their own purposes. I sent a couple of men to the abandoned gun and they brought back a couple of grapeshot shells. I immediately told the driver of an ammunition carriage to pick up all the grapeshot shells he could find. After this I felt a bit safer – in case of an attack by Vlasov's cavalry – but during the entire Belorussian operation we never encountered Vlasov's men: apparently, they were retreating west without making a fight.

At a small village, two squadrons entered battle right from the march, and started to squeeze the Germans out of the village and into the open field beyond. Our gun, under Guards Sergeant Palanevich, opened rapid fire on the Germans, who were slowly withdrawing. The retreating German infantry opened sub-machine gun fire on our gun from the left flank. A hail of bullets struck the shield of the gun and the sides of the gun carriage but failed to hit any of the crew. This was the first time our new recruits (who had joined the battery after the Nevel operation) had been in action, and they reacted in different ways.

The gun leader, gun-layer and loader were calmly firing their gun, while the ammunition bearer, Chikhin, decided it was time to dig in. Without any orders from his sergeant or me, he dug such a deep trench that he could not be seen. He sat there like a rabbit, until I ordered another green soldier, Cherkaschenko, to pull him out. During the training sessions, Chikhin had never demonstrated such speed in digging in! He was quite a lazy soldier who especially hated digging in and always found an excuse not to do it: either the soil was too hard, or his shovel was too bad, or he had stomach ache, or something else was wrong. But here, in a battle situation, he dug himself a hole in the twinkle of an eye without any orders.

Unlike Chikhin, Privates Cherkaschenko and Balatski behaved like experienced soldiers. Yes, it was just that Private Balatski who had caused me so many headaches during the night march, when he lost his horse. Right after the gun was ready to fire, Cherkaschenko ran to the ammunition carriages and brought a whole box of ammunition, sweating and swearing. Balatski was a groom, and his task in battle – after bringing the gun to the firing position – was to take the horses from the gun carriage to a safe spot. After that, his job was to stay with the horses until my order: 'Horses to the gun!' Balatski did not lose his nerve. He took his horses to shelter and then opened fire on some Germans who were firing at our gun from the flank and rear. I never expected this timid soldier – who still harboured feelings of guilt for losing his horse – to act so boldly in action. He did a great job!

A Soviet T-34 tank carefully emerged from the forest to the right of us and stopped. The top hatch opened and a tank commander started to inspect the terrain. I shouted to him: 'Drive forward, the Fritzes are fleeing!' But he did not listen to my advice and closed the hatch, electing to wait for reinforcements without even firing at the Germans. Only when a column of Soviet armour arrived did the tank drive on, firing its main gun on the move. The arrival of armour unnerved the Germans and their steady withdrawal from the village turned into a rout.

Simultaneously with the tanks, I saw the 3rd and the 4th Squadrons of our regiment emerging from the village. They were riding at a long trot. I ordered: 'Cease fire, horses to the gun!' and we rode at a trot in order to catch up with the charging squadrons.

There was a column of our armour moving forward on the road to the left of us. The firing of main guns, clashing of tracks, and roar of engines, was much louder than all the other sounds of combat. Because of this awful din it was impossible to give commands by voice, and in order to direct the gun, I drew my sabre from its scabbard and lifted it above my head, pointing the way to the gun leader and the driver. To the right of us, in the field, I saw German infantry running as fast as their legs could carry them, while the two squadrons of our regiment charged forward with sabres drawn. It was the first time I had seen a real cavalry charge and it was an impressive and unforgettable sight. The riders were slashing at the fleeing Germans right and left. The experienced riders were doing this very professionally, cleaving heads in half. The younger men, mounted on smaller Mongolian horses, were not so effective, but still I saw Germans fall from their blows as well. Fewer and fewer Fritzes were left standing on the field. Those slashed and slitted by sabres never again rose from the wet, boggy, earth.

The sabre charge was well supported by fire from our armour and field cannons. During our crazy gallop across the battlefield, some Fritz who lost his head from fear, tried to run across the road right in front of me. My horse sprang aside and I automatically slashed at the soldier with the sabre in my hand. After the battle, the driver of the gun carriage told me the German dropped into a roadside ditch and never reappeared.

It is important to say a word about our battle horses. They were real soldiers like us and well understood what they had to do, either on the march or during a charge. We did not need to strike them with whips: they themselves knew from the situation when they had to gallop forward at breakneck speed, without paying attention to firing and explosions all around. Each rider loved and respected his battle-tested horse, which in many cases saved his skin. A battle-tried horse was much more valuable to us than the best racing thoroughbred that had never seen action. Battle-tried horses never got scared under fire and were capable of fulfilling any task on the battlefield.

I must say such sabre charges did not happen often, and in most battles the riders fought on foot, using horses only as a means of transportation. When we encountered strong German resistance, we would get off our horses and fight as infantry, while the grooms (there were about ten per squadron) would gather our horses and take them to a safe spot. It was only if the Germans panicked and fled that we charged with sabres. During two years of fighting in a cavalry regiment, I only saw some five charges. However, all these charges followed the same pattern. A cavalry regiment would advance on horseback in several echelons. If the point encountered a pocket of German resistance – a garrison in a village, a delaying force, or a fortified line – the riders dismounted and fought on foot like regular infantry. If they could not break the German line, one of the forward squadrons would arrive to assist them. In the meantime, other squadrons would try to bypass the pocket of resistance and break the Germans by a sudden assault from the flank or rear. As soon as the enemy lost his nerve and started to withdraw, all riders would mount their horses and pursue, slashing with sabres and riding on till the next pocket of resistance.

Crossing the Berezina

The corps continued its dashing raid to the River Berezina. The mission was to capture a crossing on the Berezina and cross the river north of the town of Borisov, which was the key to the Belorussian capital of Minsk. A bridgehead on the western shore of the Berezina would give the troops of the 3rd Belorussian Front an opportunity to advance towards Molodechno and Vilejko.

The weather was dry. It had not rained for a long time. The first units from our corps to reach the Berezina were the riders of the 32nd Smolensk Cavalry Division. Their horses drank water from the river as early as 28 June 1944. However, it was not easy to cross the river and establish a bridgehead. The Germans put up a desperate resistance. One of regiments of the 6th Guards Cavalry came under attack from the 120th Security Regiment of the Waffen-SS, supported by self-propelled guns. A strong German task force hit our column as well, but the commander of our 5th Guards Cavalry Division, General Chepurkin, made a risky decision: he left our 24th Guards Cavalry Regiment to repel the enemy attacks, and continued pressing forward with his two remaining regiments. Two days later, we caught up with our division. Before that, however, we had had to beat off strong German assaults, during which the 2nd Squadron, under Guards Senior Lieutenant Oleinikov, again enjoyed a moment of glory. They waited till the German armour was refuelling in a forest and was thus out of action, before charging the Fritzes in the open with sabres. The charge was so fast and unexpected, the Germans had little time to react. When the German tank crews realized they were effectively stranded, they blew up their tanks. This cavalry charge was supported by heavy MG fire from mobile MG cavalry carriages, just as in the Russian Civil War, and Machine-Gunner Davidenko was firing his Maxim at the Germans non-stop, whilst on the move. Another machine-gunner, Kuhlyanovski, had his Maxim's cooler hit by a bullet. Under enemy fire he managed to find a piece of soap in his pack, which he used to cover the bullet hole. Then he tore off a piece of his tunic and bandaged his MG. Another machine-gunner, Okunkov, used up all his ammunition: he took the horse of a fallen rider and charged forward with the sabre.

After these battles were over, we had to catch up with our division. It was a hard task, as in two days they had advanced 100 kilometres to the west.

We arrived at the Berezina early in the morning. Under cover of a thick fog we reached the crossing that had been built by our engineers. The combat engineer platoon, under Guards Lieutenant M. F. Gribanov, was still working on completing the crossing, toiling with their axes, when the point of the regiment, followed by the squadron with my AT-gun, hastily entered the bridge. In those days we did not think how much labour, skill, and knowledge the engineers put into the construction of such bridges. Under constant German fire and air raids, Guards Lieutenant Gribanov always worked among his men, leading them by example. Many men from his platoon were wounded at the Berezina, but they did not leave their posts until the last carriage of the regiment safely crossed to the other side.

Right after the crossing there was a stretch of lowland, then forest on rising ground, with a hill behind it. Our point had already reached the forest's edge, when we came under rifle fire from the hill on the right flank. It was a dug-in German delaying party. A horse from a MG carriage in front of us was killed by that fire. This checked our advance. My gun and two ammunition carriages were stuck in the middle of the bridge and the Germans concentrated all their fire on us.

When we finally reached the opposite bank, I saw that the bridge was not yet complete: some planks were missing or had been broken by the preceding squadrons. In order for our carriages to complete the crossing safely, I jumped off the gun carriage and led the drivers off the bridge. After my last carriage had crossed, I shouted to the driver: 'Ride like hell!' I was hoping to jump onto the MG carriage that followed, but it was nowhere to be seen. Something must have happened back on the bridge: probably it had taken a hit from the German artillery battery that was delivering indirect fire at the crossing. I jumped off the bridge and ran to catch up with my carriages, which were riding at a long trot. But this was easier to say than to do, as the Germans concentrated all their rifle fire on me. Bullets started to whizz by. I was pinned down.

Now I had to crawl forward in the tall grass. But it was getting harder and harder to creep up the hill under such well-aimed fire. I recalled our training sessions in the artillery academy, where our platoon leader was especially strict about the creeping exercise. If a cadet lifted his head or backside from the ground, he would get a low grade and would have to repeat the exercise. There, on that field, my teacher was the enemy and the worst grade I could get was death. This is why I pressed my body into Mother Earth as hard as I could. Using every fold of ground, every small depression and hillock, I crept forwards – sometimes advanced in short rushes – all the time cursing myself for not jumping on that last carriage.

I was helped out by the missing MG carriage, which finally emerged from the crossing: the Fritzes concentrated all their fire on it and left me alone. I jumped up and ran at my full height towards the forest, to the area where I was invincible to German fire. My platoon was waiting for me there. They had witnessed my game with death, but could not help me, as they could not see the German positions from that spot. My heart was hammering so loud, I thought it would leap out of my breast. Blood was pumping through my head like crazy, and I was sweating as if I had just emerged from a steam bath.

I sat down on the gun carriage, and without drawing breath, ordered: 'Straight forward! Catch up with the column!' I quickly came back to my senses with a fast ride through the forest. I saw our column in front of us. MG carriages were catching up at a long trot. We finally rejoined our regiment.

All Quiet in the Forest

Borisov was some 14 kilometres to the south of us. It was nice and cool in the forest: the trees provided good protection against air raids. I managed to calm down from the episode at the crossing. It was peaceful in the forest, the scent of summer herbs brought memories of my childhood walks near Leningrad, where I went to pick berries and mushrooms. This interlude did not last long.

An order was passed down the column from man to man: '2nd AT-platoon leader to the head of the column!' I had nothing else to do but get off the comfortable gun carriage, jump on my horse, and ride with my groom to the regimental commander. Guards Lieutenant Colonel Tkalenko was as brief as usual in giving his orders: 'Take a platoon of AT-guns and return to the road crossing near Borisov. Lay an AT-gun ambush there and prevent any possible attack by German armour on the rear of our column.'

I picked up two 45 millimetre guns and two ammunition carriages and rode back to the road crossing. It was all quiet in the forest, nothing spoke of danger. I found firing positions for the guns on both sides of the road and the gun leaders immediately began digging in; while the deputy platoon leader, aided by several grooms, took the horses and carriages to shelter in a depression some 40 metres away. Selecting a site for a firing position, then building and camouflaging it, are crucial elements in deploying AT-artillery. If there is time, it is best to dig the trench in such a way that the gun will have a good field of fire not only to the front, but also to the rear, in case the enemy should attack from behind. But camouflaging the firing position is the most important thing. An

AT-gun can fire at the enemy's armour calmly and without distur-
bance – until it is spotted, that is.

I decided to walk with my groom towards Borisov to check the
situation. After some 300 metres, we stopped at a bend in the road
and listened . . . We heard the unmistakable roaring of engines in
the distance. At first, the growling of the enemy armour grew
stronger, but then it seemed to fade. I noted the reference points at
the place from which tanks could emerge, then walked back. Now
we had to prepare for battle.

Everyone was busy. The loaders were carefully cleaning the grease
from armour-piercing shells, while the gun leaders and gun-layers
were setting the sights of the guns. I showed the reference points to
the gun leaders and the place from which the German tanks were
likely to appear and again walked up the road, stopping every ten
steps to listen to the distant engines. The noise, however, continued
to diminish. I guessed the German tanks were driving away, but in
order to be sure, I decided to probe further along the road on horseback. We rode some 1,500 metres until the tracks on the ground
plainly indicated that the tanks had indeed turned around and
trundled back to Borisov.

I was about to report this when a rider from HQ arrived and
passed me a message from Tkalenko, ordering us to abandon the
ambush and catch up with the regiment.

In the evening, the 3rd Squadron took up the point of the regiment. I went along with Guards Sergeant Palanevich and his
AT-gun.

The road was still winding through the forest, north from Borisov
towards Minsk. Darkness fell and it was hard to see anything in the
twilight: so we had to rely on our ears more than on our eyes. At a
small clearing, the point of the regiment – a sabre platoon, the AT-
gun, and an MG carriage – stopped to wait for the head of the main
column, so that voice communication might be maintained during
the night march. The riders dismounted and chatted quietly. It was
very still and peaceful all around.

All of a sudden, a car appeared from a bend in the road ahead. It
spotted us, stopped some 20 metres away, and remained motionless
for a couple of seconds. We did not imagine this could be the enemy
– so peaceful did the lone car look, here in the middle of the forest,
without any protection. Only when the car started to turn around

did I – still stunned by its sudden appearance – shout to my gun: 'Prepare for battle!' It would have taken one short burst from a sub-machine gun to stop the car, but we took some seconds to react, and it drove away at full speed. Only then did we realize we had missed an important prey.

Now we had to ride forward as fast as we could, giving the Germans no time to set up defences. And in a madcap dash, covering some 110 kilometres in twenty-eight hours, our cavalry corps ended up assisting other units in the capture of Borisov, earning the commander-in-chief's gratitude, expressed in a general order.

Another Little Gift For You Bastards!

On 28 June our combined mechanized cavalry task force liberated Vilejko and cut the Vilnius – Minsk railway.

I now joined the 4th gun, under Guards Sergeant Petrenko, as it had been assigned to the squadron that was riding point. We rode several kilometres through the fields, trying to catch up with the squadron, but the point made a sharp turn and trotted into a forest, which could be seen to the south at a distance. We were some 300 metres behind.

As I turned to follow the squadron, I spotted a large supply column about 500 metres away, moving toward our rear, parallel to the road. It looked suspicious, so I grabbed my binoculars. I could clearly see German soldiers in the column, but they had evidently mistaken us for friendly troops and were making their way in peace. I decided to open fire, in order to deprive them of any chance of mounting a surprise attack on our rear. At the same moment, I sent a rider to the squadron commander to report my decision: 'Prepare for battle! Germans to the left! At the German column, fragmentation round, sight 10, one round, fire!' 'Shot made!' Reported the gun leader, 'a hit on the centre of the column!' I ordered rapid fire of four grenades with the shots shifting to the right and left.

Without waiting for my orders, Driver Vedernikov drove up to the gun with his ammunition carriage and started unloading the ammunition boxes. This was very nice of him, but at the same time, having an ammunition carriage at the exposed firing position of the gun was not advisable. The Germans, in the meantime, had recovered from their initial shock, and were returning fire at our gun.

Vedernikov and his ammunition carriage could be seen for miles: he was thus risking his life and the lives of his horses. 'Get the hell out of here!' I shouted to him in the brief pauses between the shots. But Vedernikov calmly unloaded the last ammunition boxes, as if he could not hear my orders or the whizzing of bullets around. Then he picked up all the empty cartridges, loaded them into empty ammunition boxes, and only then drove off. He did all this without any haste, as if he were working in a field at his home *kolkhoz*. Such was Driver Vedernikov. A silent, slow and calm man, who never lost nerve – even in the worst situations – and always performed his tasks well: be that in battle, during a march, or at rest.

Our gun continued to fire. The crew was working quickly and in a well-coordinated manner, with good spirit. Petrenko was giving orders to the crew standing at his full height, happily repeating my orders and adding some curses to the Germans: 'Here is another little gift for you bastards!' When Germans ceased their fire and started to flee, he shouted: 'So you don't like it? Some more coming for you, Nazi scum! And here is something for your damn Führer, Hitler!' The barrel of our gun was red-hot from rapid fire. The enemy was scattered across the field, leaving dead and destroyed carriages on the road. The action had been risky for us, as we had no infantry support. Luckily, the Germans did not have mortars, artillery pieces, or machine-guns in their column, and failed to set up an infantry attack on us. Thus, with a single gun, we had dispersed a large supply column. Now we had to catch up with the squadron.

Buried Alive

On the sunny morning of 4 July we approached Krasnoe, a large railway junction. According to the reports of our scouts, there was a German infantry regiment with tanks and self-propelled guns defending the place. Our squadron was given the task of bypassing Krasnoe through a forest and hitting the Fritzes from the rear. We rode through the forest for a while and then the squadron made a left turn into boggy ground.

The light horses of the squadron and MG carriages easily passed through the bog, without even disturbing its surface, but our heavy gun carriage immediately started to sink. Soon the horses were breast-deep in the mire and the gun's axle disappeared under the surface. We had to unharness the horses and rescue them from the quagmire one by one. Then we had to drag the gun from the bog. It took us some three hours to complete this rescue operation. We were all exhausted and covered from head to toe with slimy mud. Fortunately, the heavy ammunition carriages behind us had not entered the marsh. We cleaned the gun and attempted to smarten ourselves up a bit, before returning to the main road and heading for Krasnoe.

Shortly afterwards, the liaison officer of the regimental commander appeared. When he saw me he exclaimed in astonishment: 'Yakushin! Did you come back from the "other side"?' I was not in the mood for jests and replied: 'Still joking, huh? I did not come from the "other side", I came from the bog!'

While we were stuck there in the bog, Krasnoe was liberated by our troops. No longer in a hurry, we entered the village at a slow pace. It looked empty: only in a few places did we see traces of a battle just ended. But the officers of the regiment who came up to me all asked the same strange question: 'Have you resurrected from the dead?' 'Yakushin, they had already buried you! Are you really alive?' I was shocked. But later that evening, all became clear.

It turned out the 3rd Squadron, with Palanevich's AT-gun, was storming the village next to another cavalry regiment of our division. There were also infantry units taking part in the assault. One of the officers of that regiment was heavily wounded in the battle. Palanevich was bandaging him when he died in his arms. A staff officer from our regiment was riding by. He knew Palanevich and asked who it was he was holding. Palanevich replied: 'It's our lieutenant, he was heavily wounded here and he passed away in my arms.' When Palanevich said 'our' he meant that this was an officer from our cavalry division, not an infantry officer. But the staff officer thought Palanevich was referring to his own platoon leader, i.e. me – Guards Lieutenant Yakushin. He duly reported this to regimental HQ. If I had been stuck in that damn bog any longer, the regiment would have sent a 'Killed in Action' letter to my family! That was the first time they buried me alive . . .

Later the same day, the riders began battles for the liberation of Molodechno and Lebedevo. The northern part of Molodechno and the railway station changed hands several times. However, after the liberation of Krasnoe, the German garrisons in both Molodechno and Lebedevo were in an exposed position and consequently forced to retreat. Surviving civilians told of their harrowing experiences under German occupation and of the fate of Jews. In Volozhin, a small village near Molodechno, the Germans murdered the entire Jewish population. They put them in barns and burned them alive. After hearing such stories, our desire for revenge grew even stronger. Despite exhaustion and sleepless nights, we were ready to press forward, destroying the enemy until our entire Soviet land was liberated from the Nazi filth.

We continued our raid. The regiment easily defeated and destroyed individual German delaying parties, moving forward without stops. We took many German garrisons completely by surprise. There were cases when, during our arrival at a village, Germans, local Polizei, and other traitors to our country, ran out of their houses in their underwear. When they saw us and realized resistance was useless, they threw their arms in the air – to the great amusement of the Guards riders. Yet some garrisons were well organized, setting up strong defences, and putting up a stubborn resistance. This was exactly the case in a battle where I almost got killed.

Our advance guard rode through a sandy area, with young forest, and arrived at an open plain that stretched up to another village. The scouts reported seeing a large German unit there, as well as trenches at the edge of the village. The scouts dismounted and launched an assault on the village, but were soon stopped by intensive machine-gun fire. The arrival of another squadron did not help the situation. Our riders were pinned down and forced to dig in.

I was given the task of moving up to the field with my gun and destroying the enemy's machine-guns. I did not have time to choose a good firing position: in fact, there was no good position on that field – just a ravine with an open plain behind it and no shelter. Furthermore, the plain was well-illuminated by the sun, which was shining from the enemy's side. I had nothing to do but set a gun in the open, near a tree. It was easy to spot the enemy's machine-guns: they were taking turns firing at our riders, pinning them down. I pointed the targets out to Guards Sergeant Palanevich and ordered him to roll the gun into position and destroy the machine-guns. The crew had been well prepared for such situations by many training sessions in the rear. They rolled the gun into position, hiding behind its shield, and prepared for battle. It all took just a few seconds. The gun opened fire.

The first machine-gun was destroyed by our very first round. The second one, however, was a much harder nut to crack, as the German MG crew spotted our gun and rained a hail of bullets on us. They aimed well and the bullets hit the shield of the gun. It took a lot of effort to destroy that second machine-gun, but when we did finally destroy it, the enemy's artillery opened fire. Suddenly, shells started exploding around the gun. The Fritzes fired precisely and we had to dig in urgently. I saw the German fire was deadly, and realized that if we stayed any longer we would all be killed. I ordered the crew to leave the gun and take cover in the rear. I remained with the gun-layer and we continued to dig in. As it happened, the soil was sandy and easy to work. The gun-layer's foxhole was to the left of the gun, while mine was to the right. The Germans concentrated all their fire on our gun. After every explosion we peeped out of our foxholes and asked each other: 'Are you still alive?' Sand was falling from the walls of my hole: it was not very stable. After several such questions I heard a horrible bang, something heavy fell on me, and I lost consciousness.

When I regained my senses, my men were dragging me on a *plash-palatka* back to the ravine. It turned out our gun had been destroyed by a direct hit, burying me alive. The tree had been cut down by the explosion and had fallen on my collapsed foxhole. The gun-layer peeped out of his foxhole after the explosion and saved my life by running to dig me out. Palanevich and his crew had also seen the gun take a direct hit and ran to the spot. They worked hard to resurrect me, and pulled me back to the shelter on a *plash-palatka*. Luckily for all of us, the German fire had abated, as the main force of the regiment had outflanked the Fritzes in the village.

That was the second time I was buried alive: this time in a foxhole.

Victory, Excitement, and Frenzy

The point of the regiment – sabre platoon, MG carriage and our 45 millimetre gun with ammunition carriage – was silently advancing through the night. Where was the enemy? He could be anywhere. Ahead of us and on our flanks there were pairs of mounted sentries within hearing distance. It was hard to stay awake after night marching and day fighting. The night was warm and quiet. There was no moon. Sitting in the saddle was like lying in a cradle: men were almost falling asleep and losing their concentration. I was at the end of the point's column with the 4th gun, under Guards Sergeant Petrenko. Petrenko had taken part in many battles. He was a good and experienced gun leader and I could rely on him. The crew was made up of new replacements that had arrived from the Poltava area after the Nevel operation: they had already seen some action.

I discussed cooperation in battle with the commander of the point and made myself comfortable on the ammunition carriage next to the driver, Vedernikov. The monotonous movement of the carriage almost put me asleep. The horses of the column were walking forward at a quiet step. The column stopped. I could hear someone speaking German. I thought our scouts had captured a prisoner and the commander of the point, a Guards lieutenant, was trying to talk to him. A few seconds of silence. Then a hail of bullets hit us at point-blank range.

We could not see the enemy in the darkness. We could not see our own men. The only thing we could see were the tracer bullets whizzing along the highway. The fire was so concentrated and unexpected that men lost their heads. No one was sleepy anymore. Horses rose up on their hind legs, almost capsizing the ammunition carriage. In a twinkle of an eye Vedernikov and I removed the ammunition carriage from the road, making the horses jump across a wide ditch. The gun leader did the same, rescuing the precious horses from the fire. During short flashes of German MG fire I spotted the dark silhouette of Petrenko's gun on the road. As its carriage had made a sharp U-turn on the road, the gun had disconnected itself and was facing the enemy. I shouted as loud as I could, trying to make myself heard above the rattling of machine-guns: 'Crew to the gun! Prepare for battle!' Together with Petrenko, who had run up to the gun, we pulled the cheeks of the gun carriage to the sides and prepared the gun for firing. 'Fragmentation round!' I shouted. 'No fragmentation rounds here, they are in that ammunition carriage! I only have armour-piercing ones here!' Shouted Petrenko in reply. 'Alright, give me an armour-piercing then . . . Load!' I fired the gun, aiming at the muzzle-flashes of the German MGs, which were no more than 50 metres from us. The sharp, metallic sound of a shot by an armour-piercing round changed the entire situation. Of course, a fragmentation round would have caused more damage, but the psychological effect of the armour-piercing shell was much greater. After the second and the third round, the enemy ceased fire, and the riders opened up with sub-machine guns. Private Cherkaschenko crept up to the gun with a box of fragmentation rounds: the rest of the crew followed him. The situation swung in our favor. Then the gun opened rapid fire. The crew acted calmly, as if it were a training session, firing one round after another on the Germans' necks. The sabre platoon stood up and ran forward with a loud 'Hurrah!' In the growing light, they chased the fleeing Germans.

We saw abandoned machine-guns and ammunition boxes in the trenches. And in the distance, a destroyed ammunition carriage, a dead horse, and about ten Germans corpses. Behind the German defences we saw a large village. The sabre squadron of the point bypassed us. They were riding with sabres drawn. I ordered: 'Cease fire! Horses to the gun!' Now we had to catch up with the charging squadron to provide fire support. The German garrison fled. The sabre charge and pursuit continued after we had passed through the village.

The main rule was that we must not give the enemy even a second of respite. We had to deprive them of every possibility to consolidate their positions and set up defences. Only forward!

The joyful feeling of victory, excitement, and frenzy that we had when pursuing the fleeing enemy can hardly be compared. In such moments, riders and horses become one, and nothing but death can stop the avalanche: both became drunk with victory and only wanted to ride forward against any obstacle.

We finally caught up with the squadron and could provide fire support when necessary. The pursuit continued. Our corps continued its advance westwards from Minsk. In front of us lay the town of Lida. The Germans were hastily consolidating defences: their task forces of infantry, supported by tanks and artillery, built strong points in villages, and put up a stubborn resistance. We came across one such task force on the Traby – Yuratishki road, where two battalions of German infantry, plus tanks, put up a serious fight. It took a well coordinated assault, preceded by an artillery barrage from the regimental 76 millimetre guns, a mortar battery, and our AT-battery to break them. The Germans retreated in panic. We followed them all the way to the River Gatia, capturing the crossings on that river.

Now the cavalry corps had advanced too far and lost contact with our armour and infantry units. The corps commander did not want to lose time and ordered the immediate assault of Lida: the 6th Guards Cavalry attacked the town from the north; our 5th Guards Cavalry Division defeated the German delaying parties, crossed the River Lida, and assaulted the eastern suburbs of the city; meanwhile, the 32nd Smolensk Cavalry Division hit the city from the south. The 17th Guards Cavalry Regiment from our division distinguished themselves in that battle. They made a surprise charge with sabres and rode into the city, meeting almost no resistance. Once inside the town, the riders dismounted and started street fighting. The assault was so swift, the Germans failed to evacuate a whole train of military hardware from the station. The battles in that town cost us many lives. Guards Lieutenant Colonel Trukhanov, commander of our sister regiment, was mortally wounded in Lida and was buried there. Now one of the city's streets bears his name. On 9 July the town was fully liberated, and on 10 July meetings were held in all units of the corps. The commander-in-chief expressed his gratitude to the riders in a general order. Three regiments from our corps received an honorary 'Lida' title.

Private Glushan and the Twelve Fritzes

We were in high spirits after the liberation of Lida. Everyone cheered the arrival of our sergeant major, especially as he was accompanied by our smiling cook and his field kitchen. The sergeant major also brought letters from home and newspapers. Our corps had its own newspaper, *The Guards Cavalryman*, and it was popular with the men. Everyone was eating together like a family: two, three, or even four men feeding from one canteen, dipping spoons in turns. Some even had a 5 litre pot by their carriage, containing enough food for four men. No one had problems with appetite! The men consumed everything – and then asked for more. The remaining bread was carefully wrapped in towel and stowed in the carriages: no one knew when the field kitchen would catch up with us again.

I asked the sergeant major: 'How are the other guns doing? What about the support units of the battery?' 'Everything is just fine,' he answered, 'you beat up the Fritzes so bad here, they are hanging around in the fields and forests. Only a few isolated Germans are left in the city: some are surrendering; some are fighting their way back to their side.' From the sergeant major's happy face I could see the battery was indeed doing well. 'The battery commander has ordered you to write a report of your actions, list your dead and wounded, and name any men you recommend for decoration,' he beamed, 'but now I'm going to feed the 1st Platoon. I can pick up your papers on the way back. But don't forget to include Glushan on your recommendation list: he brought in twelve Fritzes to HQ.' This was news to me. I somehow could not believe it, but the sergeant major told me he saw with his own eyes how Glushan took those damn Fritzes to HQ.

I made myself comfortable in the shade of a small tree and wrote a report to the battery commander, Agafonov. At the end I included a list of men recommended for decorations. I remembered to mention Glushan and wrote that for capturing twelve Fritzes he deserved a Medal for Bravery.

Glushan was a whole story in himself. He arrived in our platoon with a replacement of men we received before the battles in Belorussia. Glushan was quiet and shy. He had a high school education, which was rare for our regiment. In the beginning, he did not show the best of himself. He always tried to avoid the tasks given to him, and the gun leader gave him a nickname: 'Lazy Bastard'.

After another extra duty given him as punishment for lack of discipline, I called for Glushan. He reported his arrival and stood to attention. He listened to all my admonitions patiently but with little interest. When I asked him what he would do in the future, he said he would try his best. This answer did not convince me and I demanded to know the real reasons for his behavior: why did such an educated man of the Red Army, in the glorious Guards Cavalry, try to avoid hard but necessary work? He said it would be easier for him to show me: 'Would you allow me to show you, Comrade lieutenant?' Somewhat puzzled, I agreed, and he proceeded to take off his tunic and undershirt: his whole body, from the neck to the waist was covered with boils. Some were full of pus. I had never seen anything like it! I recalled how just a couple of boils had tortured me in childhood, but Glushan had dozens of them! I ordered him to dress and took him to our medic, Guards Sergeant Silyutin. The latter already knew about Glushan's problem and said it was OK. He said he could put some solution on the boils, but for the rest, he could not help – it was an age thing and they would cure themselves. I spoke to the medical officer of the regiment and asked him to put Glushan in hospital. But to no avail. The medical officer recommended relieving him of hard work, and that was it.

But no vacancies for easy work existed in the rear units of the regiment. There wasn't even a clerk's job going on any of the staffs. The only thing I could do for Glushan was to put him on Vedernikov's ammunition carriage as an assistant driver. Vedernikov objected, but could do nothing, as it was my order. In this way Glushan left the battle units of the platoon and temporarily went to the rear with Vedernikov.

I only heard the details of how Glushan captured the twelve Germans after the Belorussian operation, when we had all received our decorations. The men and officers of the battery gathered for a celebratory lunch in the clearing of a forest. Our cook did his best, the food was excellent, and everyone was in high spirits. I received the Order of the Patriotic War 2nd Degree – my first decoration since arriving at the Front. As I congratulated my men on their decorations, I heard roars of laughter coming from Petrenko's gun. I decided to investigate and saw men laughing like crazy. Some were even rolling on the ground, saying: 'That was a good one! I'm dying from laughter! What a joke!' Only Glushan and Vedernikov were serious and quiet, sitting and looking at all this. When everyone calmed down a bit, I asked Petrenko what the problem was. It turned out it was Glushan's story about how he captured twelve Fritzes that made them laugh so much. Petrenko, still bursting with laughter, suggested Glushan repeat his story for me: 'Let the Guards lieutenant listen to you, you cannot hear such story in any movie or theatre!' Glushan agreed and repeated the whole story for me.

It all happened when we were still fighting in Lida. The support units of the regiment were slowly moving towards the town and stopped in the middle of a rye field, waiting for further orders. Glushan had an emergency, and he asked Vedernikov if he could go into the field to answer the call of nature. Vedernikov reluctantly agreed, adding that Glushan should be quick, as the column could start moving at any moment. Glushan walked some twenty steps off the road, unbuttoned his trousers, and squatted down. Then, as Glushan said: 'Just when I sat down, I saw Germans walking towards me with sub-machine guns in their hands, as they did during an assault. I went numb with horror. The Germans just kept on walking. They walked up to me – all tall and big men, dirty and unshaved – and threw their hands in the air! I don't remember how I regained my senses or pulled up my trousers, but we walked back to the road – me and twelve Fritzes with sub-machine guns and hands up in the air. We walked up to Vedernikov. He looked at us and asked in an irritated manner: "Why did you bring them here? Why on earth do we need them here? You only bring trouble to me,

Glushan! If you captured them, you take them to HQ yourself." I had nothing to do but take them to HQ. We started walking in the same manner, the Fritzes following me. I heard Vedernikov shouting: "Wait! take your carbine from the carriage! And let them walk in front of you . . . Hold your carbine at the ready!" And that's what I did. The staff officers took the sub-machine guns from the Germans and wrote down my details: my name, rank, unit, and how many Germans I brought with me. Then they ordered me to go back to the battery and catch up with the rest. That is the story. I don't understand what is so funny here?'

That was the end of Glushan's story, which was greeted with roars of laughter from all the men around him. Soon after this Glushan got better and left Vedernikov's carriage. He became one of the gun crew members and fought bravely – well justifying the decoration that he had received.

Are You Tired of Living?

Having fought our way through the whole of Belorussia, we approached the town of Grodno. Behind us were liberated Borisov, Krasnoe, Molodechno, Lida, and other towns and villages.

The Germans were hastily erecting defences on the eastern outskirts of Grodno, but all their efforts were in vain. Our corps assaulted the city from the north, not from the east where the enemy had built a strong trench system with barbed-wire fences. The northern approaches to Grodno were swampy and the Germans did not expect an assault from that direction. We managed to fight our way through forests and bogs, and assaulted the town with armour support.

On the first day of the operation our corps captured the railway station at Pozhene. We crossed the River Neman at noon on 13 July and battled for possession of the crucial hills on its left bank. German resistance was strong. They sent their Air Force against us. Around forty bombers attacked our column during the crossing of the Neman, and the survivors of the air raid brought me sad tidings: my deputy platoon leader had been killed as he was advancing in the second echelon of the regiment. Meanwhile, the engineers repaired the crossing time and again, until our entire regiment was over the river.

But the Germans still held several hills and put up a stubborn resistance, raining MG and rifle fire on our riders, who were assaulting on foot. The situation was made worse by the fact the enemy counter attacked our squadrons, which had lost so many men in the previous battles. We had to destroy the their MG nests and suppress their infantry immediately. But how could I do it if my gun was at a crossing, in a depression, and the enemy's trenches were high on the hills? An anti-aircraft gun or a mortar could do the job, but we did not have any of those at that moment. The chief of artillery of our regiment, Guards Major Sonin, decided to fire at the Germans from the top of another hill, controlled by our troops: 'Yakushin, place your gun at the top of the hill and shut those damn Fritz MGs up!' When I looked at the steep hill, which the Guards major pointed out to me, I immediately doubted the success of the mission.

I ordered my gun leader, Guards Sergeant Palanevich, to find a more suitable firing position at the foot of the hill. Then I climbed the slope, in order to see for myself if it might be possible to drag the gun up to the top. But the higher I climbed, the more concentrated and precise the enemy's fire became. Bullets whizzed by. When I crept up to the front line of riders, who were engaged in a firefight with the Fritzes, I was stopped by their platoon leader, who shouted to me: 'Stop! Get back, you can't go any further!' The exposed crest of the hill was in front, and it was littered with the bodies of our men. 'Where the hell are you going? Are you tired of living?' I explained to him I had an order to place my gun here. The platoon leader wanted to say something sarcastic, but then changed his mind and calmly explained the entire summit of the hill had been pre-sighted by the Germans, and he had not even been able to evacuate his casualties from the top – every attempt to do so had only added to the number of dead lying there.

I realized I had nothing left to do there and started to walk – or rather roll – down the hill, scratching myself with the stinging branches of the thick bushes. At the foot of the mound, I found my gun ready to fire at the first German trench, which was situated in the middle of the opposing hill. The Fritzes, who were concentrating their fire on the summit of the height I had just left, failed to spot our gun. We opened fire. We were soon joined by mortar crews and a 76 millimetre regimental gun that had managed to cross the Neman. Our combined fire silenced the enemy and forced them to quit their trenches. Our squadrons then started pressing the Germans into the town of Grodno. Suddenly we received an order: 'Stop all assaults, let the infantry continue the battle. Disengage, as we have another mission.' The infantry of the 174th and 352nd Rifle Divisions began their assault straight from the march.

By the late evening of 15 July 1944, the 6th Guards Cavalry Division and other units from our corps broke through the second line of German defences at Grodno and street fighting flared up in the city. The rifle units followed and the Fritzes were flushed out. Our corps and the 6th Guards Cavalry Division received an honorary 'Grodno' title.

Cursing Hitler and All His Shoemakers

We were riding towards Augustov, a town on the border with Eastern Prussia. It was nice to ride again through a forest, protected by its trees from any air assaults. Despite exhaustion and lack of sleep, I was happy, and sang a song by Nikita Bogoslovski:

Where horses would walk on dead bodies,
Where all the ground would be covered with blood,
You'll be guarded from death and from bullets
By my young love

Palanevich rode up to me and asked: 'What's wrong, lieutenant?' 'Nothing, I'm just singing' 'That's good. I thought you wanted to call me, but you are just singing. This is good!' After these words he returned to his gun. Despite all my admonitions, both men and NCOs from my platoon called me lieutenant, although I was just a junior lieutenant. Of course, it was easier to call me lieutenant, but by doing so, they were also trying to say I would be promoted quite soon.

The regiment rode forward. There was no time for rest. We had to go as far as possible. We fed our horses in the column, during the short minutes when we stopped. As soon as the squadrons halted near water, riders grabbed tarpaulin buckets and ran to get some for their mounts. After giving water to the horses, the men would put bags containing oats round their necks. Everyone was listening for the orders of the officers. When the 'Straight forward!' order sounded, all buckets and bags would be gone in the twinkle of an eye. The squadrons then continued their march.

All of a sudden, the forest was over. We were in an open field with a large German supply column in front of us. It carried food, uniforms, and whatever the Fritzes had managed to loot from civilians. The drivers and guards fled, leaving the entire column as a trophy for us. At the same moment, German fighters flew low out of the sun. They were coming right at us, keeping strict formation. Only when the first fighters strafed our column did the 'Air raid!' alarm sound. The squadron dispersed to the right and left of the road in platoons. I, with my gun, galloped to a small village with thick acacia bushes, which was lying in the distance. Riding over a bumpy potato field, the gun carriage headed for a barn. But only the gun carriage made it to this shelter: the heavily laden ammunition carriages remained stuck in the potato field. The German fighters strafed the dispersed column and we came under their MG fire. Bullets stuttered across the soil, leaving two horses crippled, which we had to destroy.

After the first strafing, I somehow managed to get the ammunition carriages under the shelter of some bushes, and dashed towards the gun. But after running several metres I stumbled and fell in the field.

The German fighters strafed us till dark. As one squadron would leave, another would immediately arrive. They did not give us a single minute to change shelter. I was lying on my back in the field, and through the leaves of potato bushes, I could clearly see the planes and even their pilots. From the very start of the war I could not stand the sound of bullets. It was hard for me not to duck for cover at every sound of a bullet whizzing by. Veteran soldiers told us that if a bullet had whizzed by, there was no sense in ducking for cover, as it had not hit you. Despite this, I still ducked for cover – or 'bowed' as they said at the Front – at the sound of an evil bullet. I was quite comfortable with bombs, artillery, and mortar fire, from the time of the siege of Leningrad. This calmness grew even more after I had been in artillery units. But it was impossible for me to get used to bullets, especially when they were coming from the sky. I was lying there with this thought: 'The next one will be mine. He will nail me with his bullets to Mother Earth.'

As darkness fell, the air attacks stopped. Despite the continuous strafing, which had lasted for three or four hours, losses in the regiment were insignificant. I lost three horses in my platoon and two men were slightly wounded. I received two new horses for the ammunition carriage and ordered the gun crew to rest. After that I went to look for the 4th gun under Petrenko. The 4th Squadron, which was supported by Petrenko and his gun, had managed to reach the forest before the air raid started, so they had no losses at all. It was hard to find him in the dark forest, but the men of the 4th Squadron helped me and I soon found Petrenko and his crew.

Petrenko's crew was resting at a forest ranger's hut. They were sitting at a campfire, frying eggs in a large pan. The external stairway of the hut looked like a bar with numerous wine bottles that had beautiful, coloured labels. The crew had already eaten and it was the turn of the drivers. When the sergeant spotted me, he ordered: 'Stand up! Attention!' I stopped him, told the men to continue with their meal, and asked the sergeant to report the situation. His description was short: 'The squadron captured a large supply column and then ran into strong German forces. We engaged them and then stopped, setting up defences. Part of the German supply column remained on no-man's land. The gun is in the line of defence about 30 metres from here. Two men are on duty at the gun, the others are resting here. The Fritzes are quiet. Please, Comrade lieutenant, feel free to try our fried eggs. There is something to drink as well.'

I was hungry. I washed my hands in some French wine – there was no water around – and started my meal. Having captured the supply column, the crew had not only stocked themselves with food and drink, but also got some silk underwear, long boots, and cloth for foot rags and horse blankets. Petrenko looked at my worn out *kirsa* boots and suggested I change them for German officer's leather long boots. New underwear and foot rags were also welcome, as it had been a month since we could wash ourselves in a steam bath or change uniforms. I could not help agreeing with Petrenko. I tried several pairs of German boots that did not fit me at all. I eventually found a pair that looked more like Russian long boots, and put them on, but not without effort. German long boots had wide bootlegs for carrying ammunition clips and were completely unfit for both cavalrymen and infantry. They frustrated a rider and rubbed the horse's sides, while an infantryman would have trouble creeping on the ground in them.

I checked the gun and the crew together with Petrenko and walked toward Palanevich's gun. I stopped in a forest and decided to change my underwear, making myself comfortable on a stump. I took off the German long boots with great effort and changed: then I was faced with getting the boots back on. I tried with all my might to get the German boots on, but failed despite all my efforts: they had got wet from the night dew and now they did not fit at all. I started slashing the bootlegs with my knife. I only managed to get the cursed boots on when I cut the bootlegs down to the sole. And this was how I walked to pick up my old *kirsa* boots from Petrenko's gun – with cut bootlegs! Fortunately, it was still dark, and no one saw me crawling back to the gun to pick up my old long boots, cursing Hitler and all his shoemakers. There is nothing better than Russian long boots for us, Russian soldiers!

Together Even Death Is Beautiful

After my misadventure with the German boots I found my battery commander, Agafonov, and reported the condition of my platoon. Agafonov told me to await further orders, as he was going to regimental HQ for new instructions. But even before Agafonov returned, a rider came with a message for me to report to the regimental commander. I met Agafonov on the way, and he told me our situation was serious. Apparently, we had ended up in a pocket once again, encircled by the enemy, and the regiment was to attempt a withdrawal. He also told me the 2nd Squadron and my AT-platoon were to stay behind in a delaying party. I observed that the 2nd Squadron was always supported by an AT-gun platoon under Guards Lieutenant Zozulya: 'He has a wife and two children in Vinnitsa,' was Agafonov's reply. I understood what he meant: in some instances, delaying parties never made it back. I reported to the regimental commander.

The morning was sunny and fine. The birds were singing – but the Germans were quiet. Officers stood around the regimental commander in a half-circle. Everyone listened quietly to the chief of staff, Guards Captain Todchuk, who briefed us on the situation, which, unlike the day, was not very bright:

- In the afternoon of 18 July, German forces managed to break the defences of our rifle units and recapture the area of Loiki – Bela, Tserkevna – Kelbaski.
- The enemy also cut the communication lines of our corps.
- The enemy's infantry and units of the Waffen-SS Totenkopf

Division overran a delaying party from our division in Lipsk and recaptured the town.

- Our corps is surrounded by superior German forces on three sides: west, south, and east. Only in the north is there a weak link with the 174th Rifle Division, which is engaged in heavy fighting and has sustained many casualties.
- The situation of the corps is deteriorating: we could be completely surrounded by German forces at any moment.
- The corps' HQ has decided to reduce our defensive perimeter.

Everyone was quiet. Our regimental commander finished the session, saying: 'The regiment will now withdraw to the area pointed out by the divisional commander. In order to provide for an unhindered march, a delaying party is to stay here on the highway. The delaying party consists of the 2nd Squadron, supported by the 2nd AT-gun platoon under Guards Junior Lieutenant Yakushin and the mortar platoon of Guards Sergeant Major Vodzinski. We are putting our hopes on you. You know your orders – fight to the last round and man! Do not withdraw without my order! Are there any questions?' I did not have any questions. 'We will fulfill the order like Guardsmen!' was our answer.

The regiment quietly and secretly withdrew from its positions and vanished in the morning mist. We, a handful of men, were left alone to face an enemy much superior to us. In front was Augustov and Eastern Prussia; behind was nothing – except for the barricades and mines that the regiment had set during its withdrawal. We all felt depressed. We knew that if the Germans attacked, it would be our last battle: we would all be killed or taken prisoner. We knew that for sure. It was like standing on the edge of our own graves.

I placed the guns in their firing positions, strictly forbade the gun leaders from opening fire, and went to the squadron commander in charge of the delaying party, in order to discuss our actions. The Fritzes were quiet, carrying out harassing rifle fire from time to time. This was silence before a storm. The battle would be heated, and the main role would be given to us – the men of the AT-battery. I discussed what to do in this situation with the squadron commander. We both agreed not to provoke the Germans. The main thing was to prevent them from realizing the main force of the regiment had left. We also had to save ammunition for the decisive battle. In the meantime, we decided to carry out harassing fire from small arms, especially given the fact Vodzinski's mortars were low on ammunition and he could only fire in battle.

I warned the gun leaders about drinking, as German carriages full of wine and other spirits were still standing on the road undamaged. I ordered the gun leaders to issue 100 grams of alcohol to the crews and forbade them to drink more. I was amazed to hear that all my men sharply refused to drink and all looked grim and tense. I thought: 'This is amazing. How can they not drink when they know we are all about to die, and there is very little we can do about it?' But everyone was preparing to meet the last battle with honour, determined to kill as many enemies as possible before being killed. We wanted to sell our lives dearly.

The gun leaders checked the guns again. In fact, while we had the chance, we checked everything: guns, rounds, camouflage, trenches, small arms, hand grenades, our grid of reference points, our readiness for all-round defence and so on. We knew that in a battle against superior numbers we would not have time to check and recheck things and that every mistake would cost us dearly. The crews were completing spare firing positions and were making roads in the forest, in order to move the guns if necessary.

A German scout plane with yellow wingtips came flying low. It was trying to provoke us into firing, thus giving away our positions. The pilot made a circle over our defences, and apparently unwilling to take more risks, flew away. We were waiting for the beginning of the German assault: but Fritz was not in a hurry and brought up more firepower – the roar of engines and the clashing of tracks could now be heard all the time. The Germans were preparing a strong armoured assault: that was obvious even to a green soldier. We ate lunch without appetite. All our thoughts revolved around the coming battle.

All of a sudden, I heard the clattering hooves of a lone horse. It was coming from the direction of the regiment's departure. Everyone grew excited – a lone rider approaching us at a long trot? What news was he bringing? I walked into the road to meet the rider. It was a liaison officer from our regimental staff. He greeted me and asked where the commander of the delaying party was. I answered that I was his deputy and would take him to the commander. 'What news have you brought us?' I asked him quietly as we walked through the forest. 'Withdraw!' he answered in the same hushed manner. His word was like the cancellation of a death sentence. I felt as if a gravestone had fallen from my shoulders. 'Well, all we need to do is disengage you Fritz bastards, and then we are saved!' I thought, taking the liaison officer to the squadron commander.

When the squadron commander heard the order, he commanded us to march immediately. The regimental commander had sanctioned our withdrawal for two reasons: the regiment had successfully disengaged the enemy, so in effect, our mission was complete; plus, our assistance was needed in breaking out of the pocket.

I proposed a plan for an organized withdrawal: I would retire with my guns some 400 to 500 metres to the hitching posts and provide cover for the squadron, which would follow me on foot. Then, when the riders reached the hitching posts, I would retire further, and provide cover while they mounted their horses. The squadron commander was happy with the plan and we did as I proposed. Firing from improvised firing positions, and covering each other in turns, we reached the hitching posts and soon the men were in their saddles, the MGs were on their carriages, and the squadron formed a column on the road.

Back at regimental HQ no one expected to see us: they assumed we were dead by now. Men looked at us as if we had come back from the 'other side'. We joined the battle for the breakout straight from the march: but it was a familiar fight, with our comrades around us. Now we were no longer alone, we were fighting as part of the regiment. Together even death is beautiful.

On 21 July the fighting reached its peak. Our corps was completely surrounded by the Germans. Our wounded had to be evacuated in small U-2 'corn planes'. The riders that escorted the wounded to a makeshift airfield were ambushed on their way back and slaughtered. Meanwhile, we were running low on ammunition. A squadron from our regiment reached a village that was occupied by the Germans. The latter thought that our will to fight was broken and assaulted the squadron, supported by a tank. When the Fritzes were some 30 metres from the squadron, the party secretary of the regiment, Guards Major Ostrovski shouted: 'For the Motherland!' and led the men into a hand-to-hand fight. The squadron stood up and ran towards the Germans with a loud 'Hurrah!' The German tank was knocked out by grenades. Ostrovski shot three Germans in close-quarter combat. The village was recaptured.

After two days of heavy fighting, the riders of the corps managed to break out. On 23 July the corps established contact with infantry units: once again, we had snatched the initiative from the enemy. Our division then rode south, chasing the retreating Germans for two more days. We again pushed towards Augustov, this important railway junction on the border of Eastern Prussia. The battles cost us a lot of lives and many wounded. On 25 July Guards Sergeant Major Vodzinski was wounded for the third time during the Belorussian operation.

As usual, all of a sudden, our corps received an order to disengage, move into reserve, and pass the front line to the infantry. That was the end of the Belorussian operation for us. In thirty-five days of fighting we had advanced 550 kilometres to the west. But if one counted the manoeuvres, we had actually ridden around 900 kilometres. We were advancing at least 25 kilometres a day, liberating the long-suffering land of Belorussia.

After Operation Bagration we had a chance to have our picture taken with officers and men who had distinguished themselves during the liberation of Belorussia. Zozulya and I ended up in the very last row, as we walked up to the scene at the last moment. Our battery commander, Agafonov, lingered at HQ and did not make it into the picture. This picture is dear to me as it is the only image of Lieutenant Kuchmar I have left – he was killed on 2 May 1945.

Our corps commander ordered all officers and men to start wearing traditional Cossack *kubanka* hats after Operation Bagration. I think this was due to the traditional snobbery of the cavalry, and a desire to look different from all other branches of the service – especially the infantry. We had a saying that dated back to the times of the old Tsarist Army:

A dandy serves in the cavalry,
An idler – in the artillery;
A drunkard serves in the Navy;
An idiot – in the infantry.

Christmas Stars

We entered Poland. The countryside looked different and unusual to us: wide fields divided between individual peasants of the Białystok region.

Once again we were in the van, entering the land of Poland ahead of our other units. It was early morning, and the streets of the Polish villages were empty – the peasants were sleeping or hiding in their cellars, expecting a battle between us and the Germans. At the last house of one village, we saw the dead bodies of an entire family – grandparents, parents, and four children – lined up on the ground. The Germans did not spare anyone. Why did they kill this family? And who bothered to line them up so neatly in front of that house?

We left the village and splashed down a muddy road. An old, shabby peasant emerged from a hut and ran towards us, shouting something in Polish. We could only understand: 'Brothers! Brothers!' He stopped at our column with tears of joy in his eyes. Then he ran back to a stack of shamrock hay, grabbed some, and threw it on one of our carriages. This meeting with a poor Polish peasant, who greeted our troops as liberators and tried to help us at least in some way, touched us deeply. But not all Poles greeted us this way. Some hid in their cellars and treated us Soviet soldiers with distrust and fear.

After completing the liberation of the Białystok area in late 1944, the corps received an order to stop for rest and replacements before the decisive battles in Eastern Prussia. During this period, we were given a relatively quiet sector of the Front near a town called Goniondz [Goniądz – editor's note]. Our regimental commander,

Guards Lieutenant Colonel Tkalenko, took all the officers of the regiment for a mounted reconnaissance to the first line of our defences. We stopped on a small elevation, and Tkalenko began briefing us. There was a 3 kilometre-wide boggy plain in front, and behind it, a range of hills held by the enemy. Despite the long distance, however, our mounted group was obviously visible from those hills, for Fritz opened up a concentrated artillery barrage before Tkalenko could complete his briefing. Soon, shells were exploding all around. Tkalenko ordered: 'Take cover!' and we all galloped into a small ravine. I had forgotten I had binoculars round my neck, and when I dismounted, whilst still on the move, they hit me on the upper lip, splitting it. That spot was sore for a long time and even after it healed, my moustache would not grow there. This upset me a good deal, for most officers in my regiment could boast of fancy moustaches, like the ones worn by the Guards of the Tsarist Army.

We received new 57 millimetre AT-guns, which had a much wider effective range and armour-penetrating ability than the good old 45 millimetre variety. We also received more mounts, as each gun was to be pulled by six horses, and an extra driver was added to the crew. We did not have any manuals or rules of firing for the new guns. For some reason they did not send them! But we still had to learn to fire them. As it happened, I had picked up a German book about Soviet artillery, which I'd found in a captured Fritz HQ. The book described the tactical characteristics of all Soviet guns, starting from 45 millimetre and 57 millimetre AT-guns up to heavy howitzers. It was funny that I had to use this German book in order to train my crews, as I did not have any manuals in Russian! That was a draw-back in our division – they either did not have, or were unwilling to issue, manuals for new equipment.

We dug firing positions for our new guns at night so the Germans could not spot them. We also dug shelters for both guns and crew. The soil was soft and we completed our digging and camouflaging before dawn. Only the observers remained at the guns in daytime: the rest of the crew slept. Although it was a quiet sector, we knew that sooner or later we would go into battle. As no one wants to enter battle with untried weapons, my gun leader requested permission to fire a few rounds: I agreed. Our second shell landed on the breast-work of a German trench, but we received such a torrent of concentrated artillery fire in reply, we had to roll our gun into its shelter and take cover. To add to my discomfort, the chief of artillery, Guards Major Sonin, scolded me for firing without permission.

There was a large cellar next to our firing position. As it was made of large stones and looked like proof against artillery fire, we decided to move in. Soon, infantry scouts began stopping by, resting in our cellar both before and after missions. They shared their vodka, tinned meat, and other food with us – they were very well supplied: apparently, as compensation for their hazardous job. The scouts always made sure we knew at which point they would disappear across the German lines, and at which point they would re-emerge. They went out on their missions in the dead of night: if the moon shone, or if the Fritzes fired illumination flares, the scouts had to lie on the ground for a long time, waiting for darkness. When they crawled back to our lines, they would give us a signal. Sometimes they would bring back a 'tongue' – a prisoner. The senior scout officer had to report to us because we had no infantry support: it was only us holding the defensive line in that sector.

One day, sheep were seen wandering around in no-man's land. This excited my boys no end, and they constantly bothered me with requests to let them go and capture the 'living barbeque'. It was impossible to enter no-man's land in daylight, as the Germans could see everything from their positions: but after dark, soldiers from both sides would go there. I gave permission to two experienced soldiers to go out into no-man's land and bring back a lamb to our side. They soon returned, and for a whole week our crews had fresh mutton.

The town of Goniondz was on our left flank, not far from us. The Germans often bombarded the town with artillery. One night, a scared Polish *panenka* (young girl) ran into our cellar. When we asked her where she came from and what happened, she spoke so fast, none of us could understand a thing. I answered in broken Polish: 'men do not understand,' and asked her to speak slowly. Finally, we managed to learn that she came from Goniondz, where grenades and mines were exploding all around, and there was no shelter, so she came to us. We calmed the girl down, gave her some food, and sent to the rear area of the regiment.

Autumn grew colder and colder. Finally, winter came to Poland. After several more marches in the Białystok area we stopped in a quiet, cosy village with a small church. The front line was far from us. We could not even hear artillery fire. The Germans had not retreated through this village and no homes were damaged or destroyed. I billeted my men and I stayed in a small, clean house. The landlady lived there with her young daughter and old mother. The women welcomed me warmly. Zosia, the beautiful and strong peasant girl, let me sleep in her bed, while she herself went to sleep on a wooden sofa. It was nice to sleep in a clean, warm, and soft bed after life in the field and long night marches.

The Polish language is somewhat similar to Ukrainian, and after some time we communicated with the local population very well. Zosia's friend, a slim, quiet, and shy girl from the neighbouring house, started to visit the house of my landlady very often. She always found a reason to visit this home – she either needed matches, salt, or just needed to pass over a message from her landlady. When she visited the house, she looked at me with a flirting smile. I liked her from the first sight and I spent all my free time in her house, drawing jealous remarks of Zosia.

I remember two distinct events that happened during that period of rest: my promotion to Guards lieutenant and Polish Christmas. Our battery commander, Guards Senior Lieutenant Agafonov, walked into our house one day and addressed the landlady and the others thus: 'You can congratulate your guest – he is now Guards lieutenant and will carry two stars on his shoulder boards instead of one.' Agafonov, the hospitable landlady, *pani* Jadwiga, her daughter Zosia, and even her old grandmother, all congratulated me in turn. The next day, the landlady arranged a feast to celebrate my promotion. The dinner was in Polish style, with lots of baked pies and pasta, which was something in between the Ukrainian pasta and Siberian *pelmeni.*

A few days later the entire village was transformed – Christmas came. Every family busied themselves with preparations for the big celebration. Smartly dressed relatives visited my landlady on Christmas Day, while she arranged prayers in her part of the house. The prayers were quite beautiful songs. My landlady led the singing with her beautiful voice, and the rest followed. After prayers, Zosia and the other young girls left to go house-to-house carol singing. They invited me to come along, but I thanked them and said that as a Soviet officer I could not take part in Christmas entertainment.

And so, left alone, I addressed the problem of how to get more stars for my shoulder boards. Now I was a Guards lieutenant, I needed four for the shoulder boards on my tunic and four for the ones on my greatcoat. But none of the officers in the regiment had extra stars, so I had to make them from a can. I put the original factory-made stars on my tunic, and attached self-made stars to the shoulder boards of my greatcoat. I was ready to leave the house, when someone knocked on the window and a choir of young voices began to sing a health-wishing song. My landlady explained that these were carol singers, asking for permission to enter the house. She asked for my permission, and let the entire gang of youngsters in, greeting them with a bow. With their cheeks red from frost, this happy and cheerful group of boys and girls, with a large Christmas star on a stick and bags for gifts, stepped into the house. Zosia and her friends were in the group. The singers formed a semi-circle in front of the landlady and started singing to her. They also played improvised musical instruments to accompany their singing. After the concert was over, all the singers approached the landlady one by one, and received different gifts from her: pies, cakes, and pastry, which she had baked for the celebration.

Then, still carrying their star, they came to me. The landlady said I should reward them for their singing. But I did not have any pastry or cakes. The landlady helped me out again and said that I could give them money in *złoty*. I had just received Polish currency and really did not know what to do with it, as I had everything I needed (a soldier does not need much). Even more so, the local population was still uneasy with the new money that we had been issued. Here I could use my *złoty* for the first time. I generously thanked the entire group of singers with *złoty* coins.

Happy with the reward, all the participants of this improvised concert, bowing and saying 'thank you very much,' in Polish, left the house. The landlady was happy that she could demonstrate to me, a 'Russian *pan* officer' such a happy traditional Polish custom. I really liked this ancient rite. After the war, when I went back home to Leningrad and told my mother all about the Polish Christmas carols and house-singing, she told me that Russian villages had the same tradition before the revolution. As I was born after the revolution, I did not have a chance to learn about it.

After celebrating Christmas at home, the whole village gathered for a service in the local church. The catholic priest – unlike our Russian Orthodox priest – was not much different from the laity. The only thing in which he differed from the laity was in the degree of his education. He was also very well dressed and shaved. He enjoyed great respect among the villagers. Happily, he was also well disposed towards us, Russian soldiers. The Polish priest in that village did not have a wife: he only had a rather young maid serving him [Catholic priests are required to renounce marriage and adopt celibacy after receiving the Sacrament of Orders – editor's note]. The service was held in the church and the congregation sat on benches like schoolchildren in class: the only difference was that they had psalm books instead of textbooks.

Our time of rest was almost over. The Front was waiting for us. We turned a frozen swamp into a firing range and had firing practice with live ammunition. The firing practice demonstrated that the crews knew their weapons well and were prepared for the decisive battles that were about to commence on enemy territory.

Pani Jadwiga and her women neighbours began talking of our leaving the village: the rumour system worked here as perfectly as it did in Russia! How on earth did those peasant women always know the date of our departure, while we knew nothing? Maybe some of our staff officers did not keep their mouths shut . . .

And so, the day of our departure came. *Pani* Jadwiga baked fresh pastry for me, hugged me, and saw me off as if I were her own son. I hugged and kissed Zosia on the way out of the house. Her friend ran out of the house when we were already in the saddle. The entire population of the village came out into the streets to see us off. They waved their hands and wished us a speedy victory. The day was cold and clear, shining white snow was squeaking under the wheels of our carriages. We were ready to go into new battles.

After yet another night march, we stopped for a short rest in another sleepy village in the Białystok area. I ordered the sergeants to take care of the horses and walked into a house. The landlady invited me to take a nap on the bed. I took off my greatcoat, fell on the bed, and quickly dozed off. I awoke with a tickling sensation on my face. I assumed it must be a fly and tried to repel it without opening my eyes, but it did not work. When I finally lifted my eyelids, I saw that it was not a fly but a young Polish *panenka*, tickling my face with a dry grass stock. I tried to hug her but she slipped away like a small lizard. Then I turned to the other side and fell asleep again.

But this Polish *panenka* returned and again tried to tickle me. I got angry, grabbed her hand and did not let her go. She got scared and asked me to forgive her, promising to tell my fortune as compensation. She took my hand and started to tell my fortune. I told her that I did not believe in fortune-telling. But she insisted, and said she would tell the truth. Then I asked her: 'Tell me then, will I survive the war?' She examined the lines on my palm and after some time said: '*pan* lieutenant will survive, but will be wounded several times!' That was in January 1945. I was indeed wounded two times in the battles that followed in Eastern Prussia and in Germany. So the young Polish fortune-teller told me the truth: I was wounded two times more but survived!

A Private Duel

While the 1st Belorussian Front was carrying out the Vistula-Oder operation, the 3rd and 2nd Belorussian Fronts were carrying out an offensive against Eastern Prussia. Our III Guards Cavalry Corps, under General Oslikovski, with its 140 tanks and self-propelled guns, and three cavalry divisions (the 5th, 6th, and 32nd Guards) received a mission to bypass our own infantry units at Ezhnorozhec, Psashnysh [Jednorożec, Przasnysz – editor's note], and capture Allenstein [Olsztyn – editor's note], in the 3rd Army's sector. Furthermore, our objective had to be secured by 22 January 1945.

The corps was advancing through Poland to the border of Eastern Prussia with lightning speed, destroying small enemy delaying parties on the way. Our 24th Guards Cavalry Regiment pushed deep into the enemy's rear in an outflanking manoeuvre on 20 January 1945. On 21 January we crossed the border of Eastern Prussia in the Brauchwalde region, south of Allenstein. Finally, we had entered the enemy's territory: the wolf's lair!

Just before we entered Eastern Prussia, Tkalenko gathered all the officers of the regiment and told us: 'I think we can send our NKVD officer on holiday now. There is an unspoken order that every soldier should follow his heart on enemy territory. If someone would like to take revenge, you should shut your eyes to it.' All officers understood this message. The Germans had brought such grief, death, and destruction to our land – there were men in our regiment whose entire families had been killed – that many wanted to take revenge. Thus, when we entered Eastern Prussia, atrocities were committed by Red Army troops – cases of revenge. But this did not last long, as official orders came to treat the local population well.

I did not hear anything about rapes committed by men from our regiment, but I can imagine that such sad incidents took place. It was mostly supply troops that did such things: they had plenty of time, whereas we were always on the move. We also had to take care of horses and equipment, which consumed much of our time and energy. However, I can confirm that many officers dated German women. These ladies seemed happy to live with Soviet officers (all German men were at the Front) and I suppose they reasoned that: 'If I live with a Russian officer, the ordinary soldiers would not dare to do anything bad to my house.'

The 17th Cavalry Regiment of our division was the first in the column that day, and as we were riding on an elevation, we could see their dark column on the road ahead. We were in the second echelon of the division. All of a sudden, a squadron of our Il-2 *Shturmoviks* appeared overhead and started strafing the column of the 17th Regiment, firing cannons and machine-guns. It was only after repeated signal flares were fired that the Il-2 stopped their assaults on friendly troops and flew away. We had penetrated so deep into the German rear, our pilots did not expect to see friendly troops in the area: apparently, they had mistaken us for Vlasov's retreating cavalry brigade!

By nightfall on 21 January, our 24th Guards Cavalry Regiment transferred to the first echelon and I, with one gun from my platoon, joined the point. We saw a two-storey wooden house in a clearing. There was no light inside. We entered. And in light of a burning paper torch, which we had lit, we saw a table with warm food on it. Apparently, the place was a hunting lodge, but the owners had left in great haste, forgetting their nice meals. We did not stay long. Soon, the point continued its journey into enemy territory.

After some 5 kilometres we ran into a German delaying party and came under concentrated fire from automatic weapons. The riders dismounted and a firefight flared up. We had to assist the riders and suppress the German machine-gun. But in order to destroy a machine-gun one has to see it! This machine-gun was firing short bursts in complete darkness and it was hard to spot. I ordered my crew: 'Prepare for battle! At the German machine-gun, high-explosive shell, fragmentation fuse . . . Load!' But the damn machine-gun was nowhere to be seen, although I distinctly heard it firing short bursts. I ordered the gun leader to wait for me and sneaked forward in the snow. My white snow overall camouflaged me very well and I eventually approached the machine-gun unnoticed. I got within a few metres from it, made sure I would remember the position, and crept back the same way. Two shells were enough to shut it up.

The automatic weapons soon fell silent too, and we captured the German position: a destroyed machine-gun and several Fritz corpses remained on the battlefield. We continued our advance on Allenstein.

We marched some 8 kilometres without a single shot, but then our point was stopped by a strong enemy garrison, situated in a large, fortified village. Another firefight broke out. The forward security force of the regiment (a sabre squadron with supporting small units) were obliged to join the battle.

The enemy garrison – up to two battalions of infantry with armour – was putting up a stubborn fight. The village was on a hill. I halted on the highway with my ZIS-2 AT-gun under cover of darkness. I sent a runner to the squadron commander in order to get clarification as to our situation. The road where we stopped dipped into a deep valley before rising sharply to the outlying houses of the village. The forward security of the regiment was in the process of assaulting these houses, several of which had caught fire, illuminating the immediate area. In the light of the flames I clearly saw three German tanks entering the village.

My runner returned from the squadron commander, and informed me that our troops had captured almost half of the village, so we need not fear an infantry ambush. I decided to destroy the enemy tanks – which were still visible – and set my gun right there on the road, as I could not find a better firing position.

The crew of my AT-gun was green and had not yet dealt with German armour, although they had achieved good results during fire range practice. The German tanks were some 500 to 600 metres from us, and well illuminated, while our AT-gun was under cover of darkness. With the very first shot we knocked out a tank. But before we could reload, the house behind us suddenly went up in flames, revealing our position. The German tanks immediately returned fire.

We had to move – and quickly – but with the first explosion of a

German shell, my crew fled, jumping into a roadside ditch. I shouted: 'Crew to the gun!' It would only have taken a couple of seconds to put the cheeks of the gun-carriage together and push the weapon downhill into a safe 'dead zone'. But my crew, which was in its first tank duel, remained in the ditch. They only reacted when I ran to the gun alone and tried to put the cheeks together myself, repeating the order: 'f***ing crew to the gun, damn it!' The crew ran up to the gun and started to put the cheeks together. However strange it might seem, the coarse words – which were not in our Field Manual – worked very well in such situations. I barked out another command: 'Lift the barrel!' And I flung out my arm, in order to show the direction for pushing the gun. But it was too late: our time was up. Before the crew could follow my command, the gun was hit by a shell from a German tank. Three crewmen were wounded. I received a shell splinter in my right wrist.

The medics ran up and started evacuating the wounded to the rear. I tried to bandage my wound with an individual first-aid kit, but I could not do it with just my left hand. It was hard to stop the bleeding in the frost, and my hand was hurting a lot. The medics helped me. Only after we used a second first-aid kit did the bleeding stop. Suddenly, I became intensely aware of the cold: several sips of vodka from a canteen warmed me better than any clothes.

Later, when my thoughts flew back to that battle, I realized how crucial are the experience and bravery of a guncrew. If only I'd had a veteran crew, the gun would have been hauled away from the danger spot without hesitation. But the surviving crew members would never again get into a panic and would always stay at the gun during tank duels.

Our battles against German armour would almost always erupt suddenly, when we had no time to choose a good firing position and camouflage our gun, so we had to fire as quickly as possible. These battles were like a private duel: but we had the right of the first shot! But if you did not destroy the German tank, it would not miss: it would kill you and your gun. One cannot deny the German tank crews were excellent shots.

On the Roads of War

I remained at Military Hospital No. 2727 from 22 January 1945 to 5 March 1945. The hospital was stationed in the Polish town of Psashnysh. My wounds were healing. One finger, which only had a surface wound, healed in twenty days; but the second finger, which had a damaged bone and joint, took much longer. They wanted to amputate the index finger on my right hand as soon as they brought me to the medical battalion, but I refused to give permission for that! Nevertheless, the joint was broken and did not work: my finger remained in a bent position, which frustrated me when shooting a pistol or wielding a sabre.

The hospital workers were wonderful, but all the wounded wanted to get back to their units as soon as possible. I decided to ask the chief surgeon to discharge me, as time was passing. He agreed, but citing orders, refused to send me back to my own unit, and assigned me to a reserve artillery regiment instead. I did not think long. I asked a fellow patient to give me a blue chemical pencil and wrote: 'To your own unit' over the order and faked the chief surgeon's signature. Thus, armed with three important documents – my officer's ID, wound certificate, and discharge order – I said goodbye to all the patients and medical personnel of the hospital and went west, to catch up with my unit. That was in the morning of 5 March 1945.

But finding my unit turned out to be a difficult task: the traffic controllers on the main roads knew nothing of its whereabouts. I should mention that all vehicles belonging to independent corps were marked with their unit's insignia. These insignia were changed from time to time. During my years with the III Guards Cavalry Corps, our insignia had been a horse's head with the divisional number under it; a horseshoe with the divisional number inside; and finally, a white triangle with the divisional number in the centre. I tried to find my corps by asking the traffic controllers about vehicles, 'with a horseshoe insignia'. But the girls – traffic controllers – could not tell me much. Neither could the military commandants of cities on the way: they were not privvy to the movements of cavalry corps, as their routes to the Front were top secret.

Meanwhile, the roads of Prussia and Pomerania were crowded with mobs of civilians from all nations. They were walking, riding horse-drawn carriages – even cycling. It seemed like a whole country was on the move. These flocks of civilians frustrated the traffic of military units. As if complying with some unspoken decree, each civilian wore an armband. Germans had a white band, Soviets red, Poles red and white – French, British, and others, had bands in the colours of their national flag. More flags were fitted to carriages and bicycles, too. Meanwhile, white flags were hanging from the balconies and windows of houses in German cities: a sign of surrender to the victors. I saw a comic scene when a French refugee or former POW found himself surrounded by several Red Army soldiers, who angrily accused him of working for Hitler. The poor Frenchman explained in broken German that he was not working for Hitler but was spending most of his time with various German women.

I did not have any strict route for my journey. In a large city – I think it was Danzig [Gdansk – editor's note] – I managed to meet the military commandant of the city and ask him about our corps. He could not tell me what I needed to know, but gave me the address of a village where, according to him, I could get precise information. The commandant offered me ration cards and an overnight stay in a hotel. Early next morning I was on the move again. Hitch-hiking and sometimes walking, I reached the village in question. There I found the Operations Department of the Front HQ, and they gave me the precise route of my corps (I am still amazed at the lack of bureaucracy in all the Front HQs in that war). From that point on I did not have to ask the traffic controllers: first thing in the morning I was on the road once more.

I met a sergeant and a lieutenant from my corps (they were from the 6th Guards Cavalry Division). They did not have a clue where our corps was and were delighted to learn I had all the necessary information. They joined me and we continued our hitch-hiking. It was good to travel together.

After journeying for some time, we decided to take a break and walked off the main road. We ended up in a quiet, picturesque area with a small lake. Behind it, we could see a beautiful old two-storey house on a hill. It looked like the mansion of a Russian landlord before the revolution.

We heard some firing from the lake. When we looked more closely, we saw a Russian officer apparently shooting at the water with a pistol. After each shot, a soldier went into the lake and pulled something out. As we drew nearer, we saw that this was a highly original method of fishing! The officer was a captain, and turned out to be the commandant of the village. He was firing at large fish, which were easily seen in the crystal-clear water of the lake. His orderly was pulling out the dead and traumatized fish. The captain invited us to participate in this sport, but when he heard we needed dinner and rest, he begged us to stay in the mansion, the former home of a Prussian general.

Our reception was truly of general's rank. We declined the offer of a bath, but happily scrubbed our faces and washed our upper bodies. The table was situated in a large dining room, with a white tablecloth and beautiful silverware. A young and slim *Frau*, in a white apron, served the dinner. The captain missed his kinsfolk, and the Russian language, and confessed to being heartily sick of speaking German. He was happy to have us as guests. He proposed we should stay for a couple of days more, promising to provide any kind of document we might need. But we could not accept his proposal: victory was near, and we longed for the Front. So we thanked the captain for the feast and told him we would leave early in the morning.

We slept in soft, rich beds, and when we awoke, a handsome breakfast was served. We said goodbye to the captain and thanked him for his hospitality. We also thanked the *Frau* for the wonderful food, and she gave us yet more to take with us, all neatly packed. After our 'goodbyes' we walked to the highway, where military vehicles were rolling west in one great wave.

We hitch-hiked the very first Studebaker truck. The lieutenant and

I squeezed ourselves into the cabin, while the sergeant made himself comfortable in the back. After some time we overtook an armoured car from the 6th Guards Cavalry Division. We stopped the truck and waited for the armoured car. The driver told us he had fallen behind the division and was trying to catch up without knowing the route of march. He was happy to meet his brothers in arms – especially when I told him I had the precise route of our corps – and we agreed to travel together. The lieutenant and sergeant climbed inside the armoured car, while I decided to get some fresh air and made myself comfortable on the turret of the armoured car. It was quite comfortable, as the barrel of the machine-gun was right between my legs and I had a perfect view of the surrounding terrain.

We drove on. There was an unceasing current of refugees flowing against us. We entered a small town and decided to take a short break for lunch. We stopped at a small, tidy house and walked in. A sixteen-year-old girl met us. When we said 'Guten Tag!' she replied 'Good day!' in Russian. It turned out this girl was Ukrainian, and had been forced to go to Germany as a servant in the house of an old *Frau*.

We asked the girl to cook us dinner. She was about to go to the cellar for food, when she suddenly cast a glance into the corner of the room, and her face froze in fear. It was only then we noticed the girl's mistress: an old *Frau* in a wheelchair, who proceeded to harangue our young compatriot in German. We had to intervene and explain to the landlady that the situation had changed. Galya (that was the name of the Ukrainian girl) was now free and under the protection of the Red Army and it was her turn to give the orders.

Galya still was scared but served lunch. We invited her to eat with us, but she did not have any appetite. She was still looking at the old *Frau* like a slave. We also invited the old *Frau* to lunch but she angrily refused. We ate, rested a while, thanked Galya and the old *Frau* for the food and left. The indignant German lady just angrily waved her hand at us. We advised Galya to speak to the local Red Army commandant and continued our journey.

We spotted more vehicles and carriages with the insignia of our corps on the road. At nightfall, we drove into Kezlin [Kuklin? A town some 40 kilometres west of Przasnysz – editor's note], a Polish town. There we met four more officers from different regiments of the corps, all trying to catch up with their units. The HQ of the 5th Division was stationed in Kezlin. The chief of staff was happy to see our little group, and ordered the commandant to accommodate us and provide food. Consequently, we were billeted in a large house, which had been turned into a hotel. A British soldier – a former POW – was on hand to assist us. He was a resourceful and good-hearted man. He showed us the different facilities of the hotel – bathroom, bedroom, dining room – and served dinner with French wine.

We had to speak bad German with the Brit, as none of us knew English and he could not speak Russian. None of us had much knowledge of German, but we understood each other well – especially after a few toasts and glasses of wine. The party continued long into the night. We slept well and woke up after nine. Washing, eating breakfast, and taking a shot of alcohol to cure our hangovers took some time, and we were ready to leave at 11.00 a.m. I started to ask around for the 24th Guards Cavalry Regiment. It turned out that the regiment had marched past the hotel in the early morning and was now some 20 kilometres from the town. I had to catch up before it was lost once more among other the units on the roads of war.

The road was full of marching troops. We were three from the same regiment. We tried to hitch-hike a car or a truck, but as bad luck would have it, there were none going in the direction we needed. But there was an entire mountain of brand new bicycles piled up at the roadside. I suggested we continued our trip on bikes and both my companions agreed. We selected our cycles, and one of my companions and I rode off. The third man, however, continued to walk, pushing his bike by hand: it turned out that he had never ridden a cycle before. The only thing we could do was dump the bikes and begin hitch-hiking again.

The first vehicle we stopped was a tractor and carriage, moving quite slowly. After ten minutes of this torture, we realized that we would never catch up with the regiment and bailed out. After another fifteen minutes we stopped a Studebaker truck – half an hour later we caught up with the regimental column. When the Studebaker was overtaking my platoon, I stopped the truck, jumped off, and ended up in a big bear-hug with Chernov, my old sergeant. He had been leading the platoon during my absence, as his official post was deputy platoon leader. A moment later a groom brought my mount and there I was: on horseback with my platoon again!

My first report was to the regimental commander, Guards Colonel Tkalenko, who was standing at the roadside, checking the march of the regiment. He wondered how on earth I had managed to end up back with my platoon. I related my adventures, including the faking of the chief surgeon's signature. Tkalenko praised my resourcefulness and congratulated me: for in my absence I had been awarded the Order of the Red Star for the battles in Eastern Prussia. I thanked him with the traditional Red Army acknowledgement: 'I serve the Soviet Union!' Then I received Tkalenko's permission to depart, spurred on my horse, and hurried to my battery commander, Guards Senior Lieutenant Agafonov. It was a very warm meeting. Here I was again with my brothers in arms.

The Peninsula Untouched by War

The regiment was moving towards the shore of the Baltic Sea, to the Łeba Peninsula [once part of Prussian Pomerania, this area – originally inhabited by Slavs – is now Polish – editor's note]. Our mission was to receive replacements and reinforcements, defend the Baltic coast from possible German landings, and prepare for the final battle: the assault on Berlin.

We reached the Łeba Peninsula without any adventures. When we arrived at Łeba town [an old fishing port and seaside resort – editor's note], it looked quiet and empty. There was no fighting in that area and all the buildings were intact. HQ and supply units of the regiment remained in the town, while our battery continued its march to positions on the Baltic shore, some 5 kilometres away.

The area around our position was beautiful. Untouched and unspoiled by war, it looked like a seaside resort: small buildings, fresh air, cleanliness and tidiness in everything. The local barracks were deserted – our soldiers, field kitchen, medical and veterinary doctors stayed there. Meanwhile, our equipment was put into big barns, and I lined up the guns and ammunition carriages in an empty yard.

While I was busy parking the guns, an old German *Frau* came to our unit and politely asked one of my soldiers if she could have a few minutes of the *Herr Leutnant's* time? The message was brought to me, and I – surprised at such a request – sent word back that I would be free in fifteen minutes. All those fifteen minutes the *Frau* submissively stood in the distance, observing our work. When I had finished my task, I went to the woman. She invited me to her house, and on the way, attempted to explain her request: 'Sprechen Sie

Deutsch?' 'Sehr schlecht,' I answered ['Very badly' – editor's note], so she started gesticulating, as if I were deaf. It was quite entertaining to see her artistic gestures and the way she tried to convey her message. She wanted me to stay in her house, and not the one allotted to me by our quartermaster. I told her I understood, but could not give an answer yet.

The *Frau* had a nice house, built in the German style. A table was laid in the bright dining room, where the two young daughters of the *Frau* were patiently awaiting my arrival. I washed my hands in a bowl brought me and sat down at the table. The food was excellent – everything a middle-class German family could obtain during the last years of the war. A nice meal, followed by drinks, loosened tongues. The landlady told me she was a widow: her husband had been killed in the war. All she wanted was to have an officer to stay at her place, as she was afraid of the Russian soldiers. She was scared her house might be robbed and her daughters raped. But the house was too far away from my battery to be convenient, and the hospitality of the *Frau* and her daughters struck me as artificial. So I thanked her for the invitation, and the dinner, but told her I could not stay. Instead, I would recommend an officer from the regiment to lodge with her (this I did, and later, one of my fellow officers moved into the *Frau's* house).

On the way back to the battery, I decided to take a different route and explore a bit. The weather was warm, there was no wind, spring was in the air, and I was in an excellent mood. All of a sudden, I ran into a small concentration camp with tiny huts made of plywood. Apparently, the camp had accommodated POWs. The entire compound was surrounded by a barbed wire fence. It was obvious that many people had been here and hastily transported elsewhere. I could only guess at the fate of those POWs. My mood was hopelessly spoiled. I recalled my father's stories about Germany. He had been an artilleryman, too – a veteran of World War I. He was taken prisoner in battle and transported to Germany as a POW. He tried to escape with a friend but failed. They crossed the border into Belgium but lost their orientation and ended up on German territory again. They were captured by the police and returned to a prison camp. There they were given two extra years to serve as punishment for their escape attempt. They saw a lot of misery there. The revolution in Russia and Germany was their salvation from captivity. My father had an excellent ear for music and a good voice – he was a member of the Russian POW choir in Germany. He liked to sing during our family celebrations, when the whole family was sitting at the table. I returned to the battery with these precious and dear memories in mind.

When I got back, my belongings were already in the house designated to me. I shared it with Lieutenant Zozulya. The landlady, a friendly old German *Frau*, was preparing my room: there was a bed with a set of clean sheets, and a set of washed and ironed underwear next to it. It was like being in a hotel! I declined my landlady's invitation to join her for lunch and went to bed. I fell into a deep sleep and awoke in the evening. The landlady then invited me for dinner, but again I declined: I just wanted to sleep. It was nice to be able to undress, wash, and then dive into a soft, clean, cool bed after so many long and exhausting marches.

Just as I was sinking into sleep for the night, the old landlady entered my room, candle in hand, and asked me if she should lock the front door? When I asked, in turn, why this was necessary, she explained that 'Deutsche Soldaten' could come and shoot me: 'Puk Puk – schießen!' I told her she could lock the door if she wished to, and asked her – putting together a German phrase with great difficulty – to wake me up at dawn: 'Wecken Sie mich es ist sieben Uhr morgens.' The landlady was amazed I could speak some German, and wished me 'Gute Nacht.' She woke me, as instructed, at 7.00 a.m. sharp, having prepared a bowl of water, soap, and towel. I washed myself, politely refused some tea, and hurried to the battery.

I breakfasted with Agafonov, the battery commander, and Lieutenant Zozulya, the second platoon leader. Agafonov gave us a task to build a coastal defence system capable of withstanding fire from medium or heavy ships of the German Navy. Agafonov had already been to regimental HQ and knew where our battery was to be stationed. The grooms were waiting for us with horses at the ready, and we took a leisurely ride to the coast. The road passed through a dense forest of fir trees. The sea was behind high sand dunes, and only after we reached their tops, did we catch sight of the majestic Baltic. The sea was calm and no ships could be seen. Complete silence, clear blue sky, and fresh air, brought back memories of pre-war holidays on sandy beaches around Leningrad. It was a real resort!

We found good spots for firing positions, marked them with small poles, and sent runners to bring up the guns and crews. We needed to build bunkers that would be the mainstay of the regiment's defence sector. First, we dug open gun trenches and rolled the guns into them. Then we built real wooden bunkers, with three layers of logs on the roof, and gunports with good fields of fire. It was easy to dig the sand, and supplies for construction – wooden logs – were nearby. The men of the battery worked eagerly.

Next day, regimental HQ sent workers from the local population to assist us. Our battery received several dozen older men, but some were sick and could not work at all. I expressed my dissatisfaction to the chief of staff, who had sent us these men. He promised to send younger ones. The following day, the workers we received were German girls between sixteen and eighteen years old. These were even worse. At least the old Germans did not frustrate our work: but these girls talked and made eyes at my men the whole time. They were scared of going into the forest with the soldiers to bring logs, and were merely flirting with them at the construction site. Work stopped for the whole day. I had to report to HQ and ask them not to send such helpers anymore. In the end, we did not need any extra labour, as we completed the construction of the bunkers ourselves: all we had to do was camouflage them well.

Our sector was quiet. There were some military ships, which emerged on the horizon from time to time, but they did not approach the shore and did not fire at us. There were some firefights between the German Navy and our artillery batteries, but they took place in sector of the 6th Guards Cavalry Division.

While my gun leaders were building the bunkers, the deputy platoon leaders and the sergeant major of the battery went to pick up replenishments and reinforcements. We needed extra personnel, horses, hardware, and fodder. My deputy platoon leader, Vladimir Chernov, brought sufficient amounts of all these, including several jerry cans of pure alcohol. Chernov was also working on settling the platoon into barracks. He got metallic bunk beds and fresh linen from somewhere, and our barracks looked more like a sanatorium! Each soldier had an individual bed. Chernov also put a table, adorned with a tablecloth, in the centre of the barracks and placed a decanter with glasses on it. This decanter almost became the source of a huge scandal.

The scandal almost happened one week later, when a general from corps HQ arrived to inspect our positions and barracks. He had a look at our barracks, praised me for cleanliness and order, and was about to pour water into a glass from Chernov's decanter when he changed his mind: 'I suppose this water is just for show and you do not change it very often. I'd rather go to your kitchen and ask the cook to give me fresh water.' I did not object and paid little attention to the incident. But Sergeant Chernov was observing everything through a half-opened door. When I noticed Chernov I did not recognize him – he was white as a sheet and extremely agitated: 'I was lucky!' he said and crossed himself. 'What's wrong with you? The general was happy!' I replied. 'Yes. But it wasn't water in the decanter, it was 100 per cent spirit!' It would have been quite a show if the general had drank it! I gave Chernov a proper scolding for such a mistake.

Perhaps this is a good time to mention alcohol at the Front. There is now a lot of talk among old *frontoviks* about the 100 grams of vodka that all troops in the field were issued every day. But in our regiment it was somewhat different. We did receive the daily vodka ration of 100 grams, but the problem was the sergeant majors helped themselves, and the vodka we received contained significantly less than 40 per cent of alcohol. My men refused to drink it at all. When we were in Russia and Belorussia, and alcohol was scarce, there were some cases of drunkenness, but our regimental commander was very strict about this and punished drunkards severely. When we entered Germany, and captured vast amounts of all types of alcohol, we drank only one glass of alcohol with every meal as a starter. This did not make us drunk, as we had plenty of food to eat. We knew about the danger of dying from drinking methanol, which looked and smelled just like vodka, so our corps commander issued a strict order that any hard spirits should first be examined by medics, and only then consumed. And that's what happened. If we found any hard spirit, we would send it to our regimental doctor and he would either give us permission to drink it or tell us it was poisonous. The doctor requested 10 per cent of the alcohol for his services. We were quite happy with the deal.

One night, fifteen officers from different units of the regiment were urgently summoned to HQ. We were ordered to evacuate the civilian population from the defence sector of our regiment. We were told to make lists of the evacuated families, and pass these lists to HQ. The occupants of one in every ten houses would be permitted to remain, in order to care for livestock and property. But I was informed that the village I was supposed to take care of had already been evacuated. I would have to 'borrow' several German families from other villages, in order to relocate them in the deserted one. I hurried to my neighbour, Nikulin, who had to take care of the largest village of all. I found Nikulin and told him I would take nine German families from him. He had not yet started the evacuation, and was happy to hear the news, as it meant less work for him. At midnight, I walked around nine German houses, told the families they had three hours to prepare for evacuation, came back to Nikulin's house, and fell asleep until 02.45 a.m. The German families were all outside their homes with their belongings on carts at 3.00 a.m. sharp. German punctuality is amazing!

The road would go through a dark forest. My column was marching slowly. My groom and I dismounted so as not to look like guards. All the Germans were downcast. They were anxious about this urgent evacuation and uncertain of their future. They stuck close to one another and trudged along as if walking to their own funeral. I tried to convince them nothing bad would happen, but either they did not understand my explanation – or did not believe it – for they still looked scared and downhearted.

It was only when we entered the empty village and I began housing the families that the Germans heaved a sigh of relief. I explained they were supposed to take care of cattle and everything: they replied with smiles and 'Gut, Gut, Gut . . .' My limited knowledge of German, which I had retained from school, helped me a lot in this situation, for I made lists of all the families, with their birth dates, in this language. I then gave the list to the Germans to check, in order to avoid mistakes. After they had signed the lists I handed them in to HQ. The staff praised me, as I was the only one who had presented lists in German: all the others, who made their lists in Russian, had messed everything up completely!

Regimental HQ informed all units that now we could send parcels home from Germany. Zozulya had some trophies and souvenirs, but I had nothing. How could we, *frontoviks*, at the spearhead of the advance, have some war booty or trophies? I did not even think about it. The main trophy was surviving and staying in one piece in deadly battles against German infantry and tanks. Soldiers from the rear units, from regimental, divisional, and corps supply units had plenty of war booty, which they took without any risk to life or limb. Even our battery clerk had several dozens of good wrist watches, which he won from the men of the battery in the 'swap with no looking' game. The game was simple: two players would hold a thing they wanted to exchange behind their backs, and if they both agreed to swap without looking, the objects changed hands. The clerk often brought empty watch cases only for this game and received good working watches in return.

Zozulya calmed me down and told me he could share some of his war booty with me. He told his groom to bring his bag. When the groom shook all the things out of it, I saw there was nothing to choose from: it was all rubbish. So I refused to take anything from Zozulya. My landlady told me she would be willing to give me some of her new clothes and shoes to send home to Leningrad. I did not refuse. The landlady and the groom put together a parcel and I sent it off home with a letter attached. I sent a second parcel via Chernov, who always picked up the best war booty of the entire platoon. The third parcel, however, was the most valuable for my relatives in Leningrad: but I did not know anything about it for a long time.

It was during my recovery in a hospital between May and June 1945 that two young nurses came to our room and told us they could send parcels home for us. My neighbours had something to send and told the nurses their addresses. But I only had a pistol, which I kept hidden inside my map case in case of an emergency, so I told the nurses I had nothing. But they did not leave and started asking about my family. When they heard I had parents in Leningrad who had survived the siege, they whispered something to each other and left. I never saw them again as the next day I was transferred to another hospital. After several months I received a letter from home. My parents thanked me for the valuable parcel I had apparently sent to them – several metres of woolen fabric, 10 metres of white silk, and sugar. All those things were in short supply in Leningrad after the war. I could not understand who sent it, and only later recalled my conversation with the nurses.

I am still grateful to the nurses, doctors, surgeons, and all medical personnel at the Front for their care of wounded officers and men.

No one asked those nurses to find out my home address and send off the parcel without saying a word to me.

The landlady would bring a gramophone to the part of the house where we stayed. We listened to the music she brought for us. Some melodies were similar to Russian ones. When I asked the *Frau* about Mozart, Beethoven, and Bach, she and her daughter told me they did not know such music.

We had an excellent rest on the peninsula untouched by war. Now we were ready for the final battle of the Great Patriotic War. Everything has an end on this earth, so our rest was also coming to an end. On an early spring morning our battery formed a column on the village road and set off for Łeba town, where our regiment was waiting. I was already in the saddle when the landlady's daughter ran up to me, gave me a parcel of food, and told me it was from 'Mutter'.

My Last Battle

Our corps had been ordered to arrive at the jump-off area in the sector of the 49th Army. We were marching in daytime, and staying overnight in villages selected by our quartermasters. The local people did not greet us as liberators, but neither were they hostile: they were used to obeying orders and so bowed to the victors. They gave us anything we asked for without complaint: accommodation, food, fodder, and so on. The supply officers of our units received food for free from the civilians. The Germans were cursing Hitler in every place and instance, saying 'Hitler kaput!' I asked an old German *Frau*: 'Why are you so mad with Hitler?' The best answer I could get was: 'He lost the war!'

One evening, three officers of the battery, including me, gathered for dinner after a long march. We started talking about our land-ladies and the houses where we stayed overnight. Zozulya was praising his landlady the most. According to him, she was young (about thirty years old), cheerful, and hospitable. My landlady was of middle age, quite strict, well-educated, silent and reserved. She lived with her old *Mutter*. The battery commander listened to our reports and said: 'This is nothing comparing to my landlady! She is so chubby that she would not go through this door, but she dances like a fairy, sings, and plays the accordion well. You have to see it.' We did not believe him and decided our battery commander was joking again. German middle-aged women were slim: they could not only slip through a door, but even through a crack in a wall! In this respect they were different from Russian and Ukrainian women. And how could she dance like a fairy if she was chubby? Agafonov did not argue, he just invited us over to his place. He had told us the truth. The landlady did, indeed, have a hard time going through doors – she had to slide herself through them. She welcomed us like old friends and invited us to dinner. We thanked her but declined, as we had just eaten. Then she took an accordion and made a small concert for us – she played and sang well.

One more march and another overnight stay – more new people. This landlady had two small, pretty daughters, five and seven years old. At first, the little girls were afraid of me and hid behind their pretty mother, but then they somehow got used to me and started to laugh at my incorrect pronunciation of German words: 'You are so big and you cannot speak correctly!' They brought their children's books and started to teach me German language. We became friends very quickly. I was well disposed towards the civilian population and children were the first to react to my good attitude.

The closer we got to the Front, the shorter were our breaks on the march. Now we were marching during the night with short stops during daylight. We completed a 380 kilometre-long march. By the morning of 22 April we were in our jump-off positions on the left flank of the 2nd Belorussian Front, in the sector of the 49th Army.

In the afternoon of 26 April 1945 the corps received the order to reach the Oder river, and begin crossing to the western bank at midnight. The banks of the River Oder were swampy and unstable. We did not have too hard a time making our crossing – unlike the troops storming the German defences on the western bank before us – but still, it was a tricky task.

The River Oder had two courses, which were actually two independent rivers: Ost Oder (Eastern Oder) and West Oder (Western Oder). The flood-lands between the two rivers were swampy and we were afraid the soil would sink under our horses' hooves, consuming riders, guns, and carriages. We tried to push forward quickly, moving the guns and carriages over different tracks, in order to distribute their weight more evenly. The Germans were firing illumination flares into the sky, accompanied by random bursts from machine-guns. Our heavy equipment was crossing somewhere to the right of us: we could hear artillery fire from there. Our column had not been spotted by the enemy and we were silently approaching the West Oder. Everyone was silent, serious, and concentrating hard. Our horses also sensed the nearness of danger and obeyed our spurs well. Orders were given in a quiet voice. No one smoked.

I remembered the following words from the order of Marshal Rokossovski: 'spare soldiers' lives, especially in the last decisive battle.' We, artillerymen, were ordered to destroy and suppress all German weapon emplacements and MG nests before the assault. The regiment received six artillery batteries (from 76.2 millimetre ZIS-3 cannons to 122 millimetre howitzers) in addition to the three organic batteries (a 76 millimetre regimental battery, our 57 millimetre anti-tank battery, and an 82 millimetre mortar battery). All these attached units were marching to the crossing together, with the tank regiment of our corps somewhere to the right from us.

We crossed the Oder without being spotted and without falling behind the main forces of the regiment. We again entered a gap in enemy defences and began our last raid into the German heartland.

Despite the fact the war was about to finish, there were serious engagements. By the evening of the first day, we ran into a German delaying force and were stopped by strong fire. Even the arrival of reinforcements could not overcome the German resistance. Our regimental commander called in the tank squadron. In the short battle that followed, they were all destroyed by *Panzerfausts* [a powerful, shoulder-mounted anti-tank weapon developed by the Germans during the Second World War – editor's note]. Time was passing by, we were supposed to move on, and we thought we would simply outflank the strongpoint. Our scouts, in the meantime, captured a German prisoner and dragged him to regimental HQ. It was a fifteen-year-old boy, crying and sobbing. The regimental commander showed the prisoner to all squadron commanders and said: 'Do you see who is opposing us? They are just boys! Now come on, drive them out of there! Victory is near!'

After a short and intensive artillery barrage from my guns, and those under Lieutenant Kuchmar, plus a mortar barrage from Vodzinkski's platoon, the riders of one of the squadrons ran forward on foot with a loud 'Hurrah!' As soon as they approached the German trenches, the Volkssturm [literally meaning 'people storm', this national militia – consisting of men between the ages of sixteen and sixty – was created on 18 October 1944 on Hitler's orders – editor's note] men threw down their weapons and fled or surrendered. The defence was not as strong as it had seemed. Our

German opponents were all sixteen-year-old boys. Despite their youth, they had been successful in destroying our armour with *Panzerfausts*, fired from their shallow foxholes. It was a fearsome weapon – a single infantryman could destroy a tank!

The Germans saw the futility of further resistance and entire units were surrendering to us. The regimental staff did not have enough riders to escort these prisoners to the rear: so they sent them without guards, under the leadership of German officers, with a certificate from our staff.

During one of our lunch breaks, when the crew of the 3rd gun was eating simple food prepared by our cook, a young unarmed German soldier walked up and asked for some food. The men sat him on an ammunition box, and gave him a canteen full of porridge, some bread, and a spoon. 'Fritz' (as the crew dubbed him) said: 'Danke, danke, gut' and started to devour the food. After his canteen was emptied, the crew offered him more porridge, and he ate everything. Having given 'Fritz' some tobacco, the gun commander invited him to stay in the crew. After a long explanation – a mixture of Russian, German, and wild gestures – the German finally understood and happily agreed.

I was absent from the 3rd gun at this time, and when I came to visit the crew, I saw the German soldier sitting among my men. I immediately asked the gun commander: 'What the hell do you think you are doing? What is this German doing here?' The gun commander answered: 'Don't worry, Comrade lieutenant, he is a good Fritz' I said: 'Do you at least know his name?' 'He is "Fritz."' 'Well, did you ask him for his name? Maybe he is not "Fritz"?' 'He answers when we call him "Fritz."' I asked the German soldier again and he confirmed he would be happy to stay with the crew. Stray soldiers often stayed with our crews for some time, but these were our Soviet men who had lost their units: this was the first time we had given shelter to a German soldier! I did not know if it was against the international agreements on POWs, but as his stay in our crew was by mutual agreement, without any pressure from our side, I did not object to such a 'guest'. So, for a couple of days 'Fritz' became a volunteer member of the crew, trying to help everyone. Apparently, he was from a farmer's family, as he could handle horses very well.

The battles that followed were so fast-paced, it is impossible to describe them. The sabre squadrons moved forward at the trot without dismounting. They did not need our artillery support and defeated small German delaying parties with their own weapons. Forward, only forward to meet our western Allies!

By 28 April 1945, the 6th and 32nd Cavalry Divisions reached the Gindelge – Friedrich – Swalde Line. Our 5th Guards Cavalry Division was concentrated in the area of Greifenberg and Angermünde. The II Mechanized Corps was successfully advancing on our right flank. The infantry was falling behind as usual.

The Front commander tasked our corps with the capture of Fürstenberg and Reinsberg by 30 April at the latest. Our intelligence reports indicated that the Germans were planning to slow down our advance with a strong delaying party, winning time to prepare a defensive line on the western bank of the River Havel. Our corps commander did not want to give the Germans an opportunity to consolidate their defences, and threw our division into battle in the area of the 32nd Guards Cavalry Division, with a mission to capture the crossings on the Havel by the end of the day (28 April 1945).

Fast-paced marches and battles began again. We crossed the Havel at Langevall and continued our advance towards Zechow, now covering the flank of the 6th Guards Cavalry Division. Again some short skirmishes, then we turned west. The River Elbe was somewhere ahead of us. The road was good, with trees planted on both sides. This protected us from the attacks of the German Air Force.

Thirtieth of April 1945. The end of war was near. It was quiet, blue sky above us. The only sound that could be heard was the horseshoes of our small task force – the point of the regiment. I was riding together with the commander of the point, a young lieutenant. A platoon of riders, an MG carriage, and my 57 millimetre anti-tank gun plus ammunition carriage followed us. In front, to the right, and to the left of us were mounted sentries. Beyond them was uncharted territory. Some 500 metres behind us, the forward security of the regiment followed, always keeping us in sight. We rode without stops, as our mission was to go as deep as possible into German territory. Our sentries were also our scouts – they rode in front, but always remained within sight. We ourselves, the point of the regiment, played the role of scouts during that forced march. Where was the enemy? How strong was he? How would he try to stop us? We knew nothing!

The tank squadron of the 104th Tank Regiment was driving somewhere on a parallel road, but we did not see them. All of a sudden, the road entered a large field. That was an airfield with aircraft on it. It was completely quiet. The Germans did not expect to see us there.

Draw sabres! We charged towards the aircraft. My gun followed the riders, but no artillery support was necessary: pilots and ground crew fled in all directions, abandoning their aircraft. There were two-engine planes and gliders lined up on the field. We captured them almost without a single shot in a sabre charge!

The main force of the regiment arrived and consolidated our gains. We stayed for a short rest in the two-storey control centre. The Germans left in such a hurry, they took care not only of our accommodation but also our catering. Our cook arrived with his field kitchen and offered soup and porridge, followed by a glass of an excellent French wine. But it was all in vain. My men were sitting in comfortable arm chairs in the lobby of the administration building and smoking expensive cigars. They had eaten the best delicacies they could find in the building and did not react to the desperate pleas of our cook to try his food!

We set guards and stayed overnight in the building. The place had everything one could wish for a pleasant stay: soft furniture, an excellent library, large supplies of food and alcohol, and several photo and film cameras. However, we were so exhausted, we merely fell asleep, without caring for all that war booty. The horses were fed and rested outdoors. We did not even unsaddle or unharness them, as we never knew when the order to mount and ride would come.

The day of 1 May 1945 came. The corps continued its offensive, with a mission to capture the area of Wittenberge, Lenzen, and Karstadt by 3 May at the latest. Before all units of the regiment started their advance, an order was passed up the column: 'Guards Lieutenant Yakushin with one gun to the head of the column!' The regimental commander had given us a mission: the second squadron, reinforced by my AT-gun and a MG platoon, was to advance toward the road at Wittenberge. We were supposed to cut the road and stop the German military vehicles that were going west to surrender to our Western Allies. The regimental commander told me as we were departing: 'Go for it, lieutenant. The Golden Star is waiting there for you.' He thought that in an ambush, we would be able to knock out a dozen or so tanks. It did not happen that way, though.

The squadron built its defences at the edge of a forest. The situation was as follows: to the left of us, some 300 metres away, a German battery was firing on our rear units. The enemy did not see us, as we were behind the battery. In front of us, about 1 kilometre in the distance, a large column of German armour and artillery was moving westward. We decided to knock out one of the tanks and create a traffic jam on the road. We prepared the gun for firing.

After a short command: 'Prepare for battle!' everyone got down to business. Even the German POW, who was still with the crew, understood the importance of the moment, and handled the ammunition boxes very well and quickly. I ordered: 'On the tank in the middle of the column! Armour-piercing shell, fire!' The grenade had a tracer, so we could easily follow its trajectory. The first one flew a bit over target. The second one hit. The crippled tank turned 180 degrees on the road and stopped. The column stopped. Some vehicles tried to bypass the knocked out tank: the rest tried to turn round on the road.

All we had to do now was secretly – and speedily – change our firing position. We realized that as soon as we opened fire, the German battery would turn their guns on us and fire over the open sight. But this did not happen. The German crews fled from their guns at our very first shot! But behind the enemy battery was a camouflaged assault gun, lying in ambush. It had spotted our first shot and opened fire.

The first grenade exploded some 10 metres to the right from us. The second shot was a direct hit, which destroyed our gun. My gun commander was killed outright and I was wounded – my third wound at the Front. Only the gun-layer and the grooms remained more or less intact. Under covering fire from the squadron, the grooms took all the wounded to a safe spot, where we were all bandaged. Using 'Fritz' as my support, I walked to a forest road. Our regiment, led by the commander and his staff, was moving towards me with banners flying. The first flag was the Order of the Red Banner, which the regiment received during the Civil War in Kotovski's Brigade. The second flag was the Guards Banner, which the regiment received for the Yelets operation in December 1941. It was the first time during the whole war when one could see such a sight: the regimental commander and his staff, with banners flying, riding to battle in bright daylight.

Our group completed its mission and managed to prevent the German breakthrough to the west. Later, I looked at the tank we had knocked out. The shell had penetrated the side armour of the tank and apparently hit the ammunition store. The turret was turned to the side, the main gun was in its lowest position. Behind the tank were abandoned German vehicles. That was my last battle.

Luckily, the splinter that hit my left calf only tore muscles without damaging any bones. But the wound was large: some 6 by 10 centimetres. The driver took me and the assistant scout platoon leader to the medical platoon of our regiment. They made tetanus injections there, bandaged us, and sent us to the medical squadron. I only remained there one day, before being sent to Evacuation Hospital No. 124, where they took my details for the official records: putting by mistake 3 May, instead of 1 May, as the date of my receiving the wound.

The Evacuation Hospital was stationed in a forest in a large, wooden, two-storey building. There were metallic beds with wardrobes next to them. There were about fifteen casualties in one room: most of the wounded could walk themselves. I was not allowed to walk, even with crutches. It was quiet around the hospital. One could not hear any firing – not even artillery. Only the calming whispers of the wind in the fir trees, through an open window. Despite pain, it was nice to be in a clean, soft bed. The only thing that bothered us was the groups of stray Germans and Waffen-SS men still wandering in the forests. We did not have any guards and there were no units stationed nearby. Our wooden building needed just one burst of incendiary bullets from a sub-machine gun to catch fire and burn like a torch.

Before we could think up any plan of defending ourselves in case of a German assault, a firefight erupted next to the hospital. We could hear the stuttering of all sorts of small arms fire. The sound of battle grew: approaching our building, as it seemed to us. No one wanted to be killed or burnt alive in the last days of the war: the room was empty in a second. The wounded fled from the building, following the medics, who had run away earlier. Myself and another immobilized man were the only ones left in the room. We could not walk but we could crawl. I crept off my bed and took my pistol out of my map case (I should mention that I would always take my pistol out of its holster after being wounded, and put it into my map case, in order to keep it with me in hospital – officers were searched in the hospitals and pistols taken away from them, but they never searched the map cases). So, just like that, in my underwear and with a pistol in my hand, I sneaked out of the room and then out of the building. I had to crawl as far as possible from the wooden building, which could catch fire at any moment. I crawled some 30 metres from the building and hid in the bushes. It was the evening of 9 May 1945.

The forest was dark. The firefight did not abate. The sound of shooting came closer and closer. All of a sudden, a Soviet soldier ran into the clearing in front of me. He lifted his sub-machine gun and fired a long burst into the air. I shouted: 'Stop! Where are the Germans?' The soldier was dumbfounded. Only when he saw me, there in bushes, did he shout back with joy and jubilation: 'What Germans? Victory! Victory!' He fired several more bursts into the air before running off to tell his comrades the great news. We were all waiting for victory, but we did not expect it would come so quickly and so unexpectedly. I crawled back into the building, back into the room. It was empty but for the second badly wounded man who could not walk, and who was hiding under his bed. I returned my pistol to its lair in the map case. Then I began to shout: 'Hurrah! Hurrah! Victory! Victory . . .'

Epilogue

For the Red Army's final assault on Berlin, three Soviet Fronts had been assigned, totalling some two and a half million men, 6,000 tanks, 42,000 guns, and over 7,000 aircraft. On 16 April 1945, the First Belorussian Front, under Marshal Zhukov, launched a dawn attack, later supported by Marshal Konev's First Ukranian Front. On 19 April Zhukov reached the outskirts of Berlin, while Konev pushed south of the city. By 25 April Berlin was surrounded and on the same day, the Second Belorussian Front, under Marshal Rokossovsky, pierced the III Panzer Army's line near Stettin. Hitler, hiding in his Berlin bunker, continued to deploy make-believe armies, while the all-too real Red Army annihilated the city's defences. By 1 May Hitler was dead, having committed suicide, and the Soviet Red Banner was fluttering above the Reishstag. On 2 May Berlin officially surrendered to the Red Army, and on 8 May Field Marshal Keitel signed a document of unconditional surrender.

Yakushin and his fellow patients celebrated Victory Day in the Evacuation Hospital, getting drunk on vodka and pure spirit. The following day, he was sent east to Field Mobile Hospital 93, a well equipped unit accommodated in a former German hospital. He was then moved to another hospital at Prenzlau, remaining there until 6 June 1945. On that day, having received a letter from his battery commander, Agafonov, advising him to rejoin his unit and collect an Order of Alexander Nevski (awarded for the last battles in Germany) that was waiting for him, Yakushin quit hospital and hitch-hiked to the Polish border. After being reunited with his regiment, now stationed in Poland, Yakushin received home leave, and set off for Leningrad by train in late June:

The train was so overcrowded, no one could even turn. I was squeezed between a pretty Polish *panenka* and the girlfriend of an unknown regimental commander. That was quite nice, much nicer than being squeezed between tobacco-smelling Polish travellers, with their huge travel bags. Most of the Polish passengers got off at stops before the border: at last there was more room in the wagons.

The train stopped before the Soviet border and did not budge any further. Accompanied by two other officers, I went to the steam engine to find out the reason for the delay. The only person present in the steam engine was a stoker, who told us the engine-driver and his assistant had gone to have a beer. We followed the stoker's directions, and found the engine team propping up a bar, blithely drinking beer, engaged in an apparently endless conversation. We had some beer and went back to the train. An officer approached us and warned us that Soviet border guards were confiscating all handguns from officers. I was not happy about this! I put my pistol into my map case – just like I used to do when going to hospital. When the border guards came, I showed them my empty pistol holster, and told them I left the pistol at the regiment.

Eventually, the engine driver and his assistant returned to the train, a long whistle sounded, and we crossed the border into the Soviet Union. I was back in my country, alive and healthy – not taking into account my last wound, which had not yet healed – and going home to Leningrad!

In the evening we arrived in Lvov, the end of the line for this Polish train. The station was teeming with people. There were no tickets anywhere. People were sleeping in the waiting hall of the station, on the chairs, and on the floor. Most of the stranded travellers were military personnel. Bad news: people had been waiting here for three days and there was no hope of getting tickets. We spent the night sleeping on our luggage.

Next day I wandered round Lvov, admiring its architecture. The city did not look too damaged by war to me. I returned to the station and saw that only senior officers – from majors upwards – could get tickets for Moscow. I decided to continue my journey on a freight train. Half an hour later, I was on my way to Kiev. I fell asleep to the monotonous sound of the train's wheels, eating up the track.

Next to me was a teenager, a boy about sixteen years old. All of a sudden, this boy became agitated and pulled my sleeve, pointing at an open platform on the next railway carriage. There was a man standing there, wearing a military uniform without insignia. 'Look! He will steal a case now!' I did not believe the boy and told him that military personnel were not thieves or robbers: but I prepared my pistol for firing, just in case, and hid it under my greatcoat. I fell asleep again. The boy nudged me once more. I opened my eyes and saw the man in the uniform jump off the train with someone's case. I pulled the pistol out and fired. The 'military' man rolled down the railway embankment together with the case.

After another 10 kilometres we arrived at Fastov, a large railway station. The conductor told me the stop would last about thirty minutes. I got off the train in order to stretch my legs. There was a military patrol and I informed them of the incident with the uniformed man stealing the case. A lieutenant, the chief of the patrol, told me it was a common thing. He added that whole gangs of armed men would stop trains in this area, robbing passengers. It all sounded so alien to us, *frontoviks*. We could not imagine that while good men were at the Front, fighting for the country, some bastards in the rear were robbing helpless passengers.

We arrived in Kiev after some time. Unlike in Lvov, the train station here was still in ruins. The ticket office was closed, besieged by a huge queue. I went to the city, had lunch in a canteen, and returned to the station. There were no tickets for the overcrowded transit trains to Moscow. I spent one more night at this railway station.

In the morning, I heard a message over the loudspeaker: 'A train to Moscow is being formed . . .' Such trains were dubbed '500th Happy Trains'. They were made of railway trucks for cattle, equipped with makeshift wooden bunk beds for passengers. Military personnel did not even need tickets for such trains. The train moved slowly, stopping at every station to let other, more important trains overtake it. There were not so many travellers in my truck. It was nice to sleep on the upper bunk bed. The sliding doors of the truck were opened and the air was full of the fragrance of herbs. My dear motherland! The only thing bothering me was I only had fifteen days of leave, regardless of how long it would take me to get to Leningrad.

Two days later I was in Moscow. I rushed into the metro and went straight to Leningrad station. It was strange, but there was no queue in front of the ticket office. I presented all my papers and expected to hear the standard phrase: 'sold out'. But I got the ticket immediately, and the ticket conductor told me to hurry, as the Leningrad train was leaving in fifteen minutes. I ran to the train. The tortures of travelling in overcrowded trains were over: I was in a comfortable compartment that would take me to my home city.

When I got off the train at Moscow station in Leningrad, I thought for a long time how I should go home. It had been three and a half years since I left my city. Those three and a half years seemed an eternity. The war was the reason. I left the city a schoolboy and had come back a respectable officer, a *frontovik*, with three decorations earned in battle. In order to be on the safe side, I asked a pedestrian how to get to Pokrovskaya Square, took a tram, and rode through my dear city. Passengers on the tram saw I was a *frontovik* and almost half of the passengers walked up to me, asking about their fathers, sons, or brothers, who had gone to war. They hoped I had served in the same unit as their relatives, or had heard something of their units. Women were asking me when their loved ones would come back home. A hail of questions fell on me from all sides. I was one of the first *frontoviks* to reach Leningrad on leave. But what could I tell them, my dear fellow citizens of Leningrad, women who were missing their loved ones so much? There were so many fronts, armies, corps, divisions, and regiments in that war . . .

But there were almost no *frontoviks* among military personnel in Leningrad in June 1945. Women were waiting for their men to come back. The issuing of leave to officers and men had only just started, so it was understandable that women attacked any *frontovik* with a host of questions. Even when I got off the tram, some women followed me, continuing to ask after their relatives. They really envied my parents, who would soon see their son safe and sound. My family – my mother, father, and younger brother, did not know anything about my leave. I could not inform them beforehand, as I got this leave unexpectedly. The only thing they knew from my last letter was that I was alive, wounded in the last battle, and recovering in a hospital in Poland.

I walked up to my home, climbed the staircase, and rang the door bell. A strange woman opened the door and asked me: 'who are you looking for?' She was our new neighbour, who did not know me. I heard the familiar steps of my mother behind her back. My brother also walked up to the door. It was an indescribable meeting. We all wept with joy, hugged and kissed each other. All the neighbours ran to the hall to see a living *frontovik*.

Index